TELEVISION AS AN INSTRUMENT OF TERROR

Essays on Media, Popular Culture, and Everyday Life

Arthur Asa Berger

Transaction Books
New Brunswick, New Jersey

Copyright © 1980 by Transaction, Inc.
New Brunswick, New Jersey 08903

All rights reserved under International and Pan-American Copyright
Conventions. No part of this book may be reproduced or transmitted in
any form or by any means, electronic or mechanical, including
photocopy, recording, or any information storage and retrieval system,
without prior permission in writing from the publisher. All inquiries
should be addressed to Transaction Books, Rutgers—The State University, New Brunswick, New Jersey 08903.

Library of Congress Catalog Number: 78-55942
ISBN: 0-87855-708-3 (paper)
Printed in the United States of America

Library of Congress Cataloging in Publication Data

Berger, Arthur Asa, 1933-
    Television as an instrument of terror.

    1. Mass media—Addresses, essays, lectures. 2. Pop-
ular culture—Addresses, essays, lectures. I. Title.
P91.B45   301.16'1   78-55942
ISBN 0-87855-708-3

To my wife, Phyllis, and my children, Miriam and Gabriel

CONTENTS

An Introduction, of Sorts ix
Acknowledgements xi

Part 1: Theoretical Concerns 1
Am I a Siamese Twin? 3
Popular Culture for Pleasure and Profit 13
Discovering Pop Culture 27
The Ugly Ones: Images of Americans in Asia and Elsewhere ... 33

Part 2: Comics 37
Politics in the Comics 39
Unflattering Definitions: Significant Stereotypes of
    Americans in European (French and Italian) Comics 53
Dagwood in the American Psyche 75

Part 3: Television 81
Television as an Instrument of Terror: A Theoretical
    Perspective 83
The Last Word (Television Columns from *Focus* Magazine) 99
The Six Million Dollar Man 113

Part 4: Advertising 117
Analyzing the Advertisement 119
Pale Horse, Pale Bather: An Analysis of the White Horse
    Advertisement with the Lady in the Bath 129
Women and Advertising: Selling with Sex 135
The Wednesday Specials as Theatre of the Absurd 145

Part 5: Humor 149
Humor as a System of Communication 151
Huck Finn as an Existential Hero: Making Sense of Absurdity .. 157
The Great Game of Academic 167

Part 6: Fads, Foods, Artifacts 171
   Status in Foods, or Cuisines as Codes 173
   Yanqui Bread: The Great White Way 177
   Some Thoughts on Threads................................. 179
   Varieties of Topless Experience 183

Part 7: Amongst the UK 187
   Hamburger Heaven 189
   London's Underground as a Work of Art 193
   Upstairs, Downstairs 197
   The Pub Life is Changing 201
   English Encounters 203

An Introduction, of Sorts

It is, or should be, common knowledge in academia that Arthur Asa Berger is not for real. Indeed, the true identity of this red-haired elfin imposter, who is to popular culture what Frankenstein is to plastic surgery, may never truly be known. But though his range of interests is far too varied and eclectic for one mere mortal, he has been incredibly successful in protecting his anonymity while flaunting his perceptions within the pages of a steady stream of volumes, with which he has been subtly proselytizing generations of unsuspecting readers.

No delicate nuance in our culture seems to escape the eagle eye or scratchy pen-point of this sardonic spectator in the arena of life. Whether dealing with such earth-shattering subjects as "Dagwood in the American Psyche" or "Huck Finn as an Existential Hero," Berger strikes again and again with his pithy pronouncements and offbeat observations. Long have I known this titan of the trivial, this capricious chronicler of the trends and mores of our time; and long have I marvelled at his perception and his wit.

Now, for the first time, Berger — the burgeoning Boswell of pop culture — presents a cataclysmic collection of his essays, some of which have appeared in the *Journal of Popular Culture*, the *Journal of Communication, Human Behavior, Rolling Stone, Society*, the *San Francisco Chronicle*, and others of their ilk. Here, within these pages, you'll be assaulted by a vast cornucopia of daring concepts, dazzling critiques, and dramatic conclusions. Like 'em or lump 'em — you won't be bored!

STAN LEE
(Publisher, Marvel Comics)

Acknowledgements

It is very satisfying for me to present this volume of collected essays —
some previously published and others appearing here for the first time. I
am grateful to Irving Louis Horowitz and his cooperative colleagues at
Transaction Books for their assistance with the book. And I am grateful
to the editors of such journals as *Rolling Stone*, the *Journal of Communication*, the *Journal of Popular Culture* and *Focus* for publishing my
work in the first place. I also appreciate, to a certain degree, the "Introduction, Of Sorts" which my good friend Stan Lee wrote for this
book. At least I think I do? And I think that Stan Lee is a good friend?
You have read his introduction and can decide for yourself.

How I ended up writing about popular culture and the mass media is,
as they say, "a puzzlement." I spent my undergraduate years reading
Victorian literature — endlessly, it seems. I was a literature student and
my work in criticism may have given me a point of view which I've applied to comics and television, amongst other things. But I was also a
philosophy student and dabbler in the social sciences as well as an artist.
When I went to graduate school in American Studies at the University of
Minnesota, I moved into political theory, with Mulford Q. Sibley, and
intellectual history, with David Noble. I wrote a term paper on Li'l
Abner for Sibley in a political theory course and, once started on the subject, I continued on to do my doctorate on Li'l Abner . . . and to explore
the vast and endlessly growing subject called popular culture, mass
culture, the public arts and now, most recently, mass-mediated culture.

I have benefited from the ideas (and in some cases the friendship) of
the following people and would like to acknowledge my indebtedness:
Sigmund Freud, Bronislaw Malinowski, Mary Douglas, Jean-Marie
Benoist, Umberto Eco, Marshall McLuhan, Leslie Fiedler, Alan
Gowans, David Manning White, John Cawelti, Roland Barthes, Edgar
Morin, Michael Real, George Gerbner, Aaron Wildavsky, Harry
Geduld, Martin Grotjahn, S.I. Hayakawa, Ernest Dichter, Claude Lévi-
Strauss, Michel Foucault, Vladimir Propp, Gregory Bateson, Ferdinand

de Saussure, Stanley Milgram, Johan Huizinga, Richard Hoggart, Herbert Hendin, Ernest Dichter, Herb Zettl, Stuart Hyde, and Charles "Sparky" Schulz. There are many others too.

The Faculty Manuscript Service at San Francisco State University typed the manuscript for this book with their typical zeal for perfection.

Grateful acknowledgement is made to the following publishers for permission to use copyrighted material:

"Some Thoughts on Threads," published by permission of *California Living Magazine*, the *San Francisco Examiner*.

"Politics in the Comics," published by permission of *Crimmer's: The Journal of Narrative Arts*, Spring 1976.

"The Last Word," published by permission of *Focus* Magazine, KQED Television, San Francisco, Ca.

"Discovering Pop Culture," "Dagwood in the American Psyche," and "English-American Crosscurrents," published by permission of *Human Behavior* magazine.

"Am I a Siamese Twin," "Analyzing the Advertisement," "Varieties of Topless Experience," published by permission of the Bowling Green State University Popular Press, *The Journal of Popular Culture* and *Popular Culture Methods*.

"Huck Finn as an Existential Hero," published by permission of Cyril Clemens, editor, *Mark Twain Journal*.

"Hamburger Heaven," published by permission of *New Society*. This article first appeared in New Society London, the weekly review of the Social Sciences.

"Yanqui Bread: The Great White Way," from *Rolling Stone* © 1974 by Rolling Stone Magazine. All Rights Reserved. Reprinted by Permission.

"London's Underground as a Work of Art," "Pub Life," published in *This World* magazine, the *San Francisco Chronicle*.

"The Great Game of Academic," published in the *Subterranean Sociology Newsletter*.

"Upstairs, Downstairs," "The Six Million Dollar Man," published in *Society*, Transaction, Inc.

Myth and Modern Man by R. Patai, Prentice-Hall.

Sociology by Horton and Hunt and *The Female Eunuch* by Germaine Greer, McGraw-Hill Books.

Culture Against Man by J. Henry, Random House.

The Responsive Chord by A. Schwartz, Doubleday & Co.

The Consciousness Industry by H. Enzenberger, *Seabury Press*.

Television as an Instrument of Terror

Part 1

Theoretical Concerns

Am I a Siamese Twin?

OR: Confessions of an Unclassifiable Image
OR: "All I am saying . . . is give pop a chance."

I

I ripped open Fishwick's letter and read the contents:

> Can YOU make an essay called: AM I A SIAMESE TWIN? It would pick up on the contention of our book that popular culture and the new journalism are Siamese twins . . . that new writers (like Wolfe, Talese, Hunter Thompson — yes, and old A.A. Berger) are true hybrids . . . their style reflects their popular culture and vice versa.
>
> Should you accept this assignment, Arthur, the academic community will accept no responsibility for you in the event you are captured. Good luck, Arthur. This letter will self-destruct in five seconds.

There was a sudden "poof" and the letter went up in flames. "Much cheaper than tape recorders," I thought. At that moment I heard a faint buzz and the light above "M's" door glowed.

" 'M' wants you," said Miss Anthrope, our shapely and slightly senile secretary, and with that I breezed in the door. He was bouncing around, as usual. I had long suspected he was made of rubber — and now I was almost certain.

"We're having trouble with this new journalism business, Arthur," he said, "and as a B2689, a licensed misologist, I want you to have a crack at it."

I frowned . . . it wasn't *quite* my line. Or was it? Maybe "M" knew something I didn't?

3

"What are you typing with nowadays?" he asked.

"My trusty *Smith-Corona Deluxe Portable*."

He smiled. I noticed he was busy Xeroxing letters and stuffing them in envelopes. His image was also getting fainter . . . and he started looking like . . . was it a chimp?

"That won't do. It's been skipping a lot and I don't like your face," he replied. ("Let's not get personal," I thought.)

He pressed a button and immediately a clean-shaven but stooped man entered the room, pulling a table on which lay a shrouded typewriter.

"What have you brought Berger?" asked "M."

"We have a fine antique *Royal* office machine," he replied. "New roller, cleaned, and . . . *very* reliable." He trilled the "r" in his "very" . . . typical British civil servant.

"All right Arthur —" said "M," "give it a try."

I sat down and let my fingers play over the keyboard. It was smooth and firm and responded instantly. I typed "Now is the Time for All Good Men to Come to the Aid of Their Country." I still fancied my old *Smith-Corona* but "M" had *that* look on his face.

"I give up," I said. I went home, grabbed a couple of *Twinkies* and had a *Dr. Pepper* on ice, not shaken, with a teaspoon of light *Karo Syrup*, and sat down at my new typewriter.

II

Until the age of forty I was secure in the belief that I was an "unclassifiable image," as a friend once put it. After all — I had a degree in American Studies, taught in an "interdisciplinary" department, and wrote about popular culture. I lacked an academic identity — and luxuriated in my freedom. I told sociologists I was an anthropologist; I told anthropologists I was a psychologist; I told psychologists I was a political scientist; I told political scientists I was a sociologist. Nobody could catch me in their little paradigms, let alone "place" me.

And then one day it dawned upon me that more than anything else I was a secret agent, a "sociological" (in the widest sense of the term) subversive, who sought the secrets buried in our commonplaces. (I'm after the "national secrets" and the hidden beliefs and assumptions of the people in America [and elsewhere]; and my problem is made difficult because what I'm looking for is not locked away in some safe, but is all about me — rendered invisible by its all-pervasiveness. In particular I'm looking for "insights," which I take to be the recognition of meanings and relationships that were not seen before.)

I was out to crack the "culture codes" and was having a marvelous time, lurking in the shadows of the collective consciousness, when I had an identity crisis. I looked in the mirror and instead of seeing very little of myself, instead of seeing an unclassifiable image, I saw a strange figure before me — two Arthur Asa Bergers, joined to one another! I rushed to the dictionary, and looked up *Siamese Twin*:

[fr. Chang 1874 and Eng 1874 congentially united twins born in Siam] 1. one of a pair of congenitally united twins in man or lower animals 2. a double monster.

What could Fishwick have meant? Which definition? Or both? Was it his fault? In any case it didn't take me long to figure out what that other image was doing there, for it represented my "other nature," my alter-image, *Arthur Prime* "the new journalist" who had insinuated himself into my life and psyche.

Ah yes, the dialectic; and the problem of identity. Was this second self to be interpreted as a manifestation of *de-individuation* or, instead, of self-awareness and the recognition of my real *double* self? Was this the new me or did it represent some kind of a revolutionary assertiveness by one facet of my personality, or one element in my intellectual constellation, striving for supremacy? Was *Arthur Prime* saying to Arthur "Look, you've always thought of yourself as a pop culturist (whatever that is) but don't you realize, friend, that you are also a new journalist? Can't you see that *what* you write about, and the *way* you write about it, can be described as the new journalism as well as popular culture? And if so, I demand a bit of recognition as being a legitimate element of your identity — as a person and a scholar."

"What chutzpah," I thought, "what nerve. If every element of my intellectual repertoire demanded a separate bodily manifestation, I'd be a division, and I'd be lost in my multiplicity." This would have to stop.

"No you don't," I said to *Arthur Prime*. "Who the hell do you think you are? You've got no special claim to a separate body and I'd be happy if you'd pop off . . ."

"If you can convince me I will, Arthur," he said, "and if you can't, I won't."

Already in my mind I was pondering the *real* significance of my transmogrification. Was I interpreting *Arthur Prime* incorrectly? Was he another aspect of my calling or . . . a reaffirmation of my original notion that I was a secret agent? Did he signify that I was — a *double* secret agent, so that I could, legitimately, be on both sides of every issue at the same time? Or was he an aspect of my work calling attention to himself?

"The problem you pose," I said to him "is that you assert that each aspect of a person's intellectual perspective has the right to a separate and distinctive embodiment . . . and that is ridiculous . . . just as it would be ridiculous if each aspect of somebody's personality asserted its right to a separate status. Recall what Dryden wrote about an English duke, which went something like this:

> A man so various, that he seemed to be
> Not one, but all mankind's epitome:
> Stiff in opinions, always in the wrong;
> Was everything by starts, and nothing long;
> But, in the course of one revolving moon,
> Was chemist, fiddler, statesman, and buffoon:
> Then all for women, painting, rhyming, drinking,
> Besides ten thousand freaks that died in thinking.

That is, we're all a Gestalt . . . and even if you are *part* of me, you have no right to assert yourself over other aspects of my academic or intellectual identity."

"You acknowledge," *Arthur Prime* said, "that you are, to a degree, a new journalist?"

"Yes."

"But what you claim is that new journalism isn't that much different from the work *many* pop culturists and social scientists do? Is that what you are saying?"

"Of course. You don't *have* to reject the null hypothesis to be a social scientist. You don't *have* to know all about coefficients of correlation and standard deviations, you need not be an expert in systems theory, multivariate analysis or any of that stuff. And likewise, there are many approaches you can use in writing about popular culture."

"Well, then, what's the difference between popular culture and the new journalism?" asked *Arthur Prime*.

"A matter of style and emphasis more than anything else," I replied. "You must remember that you are talking to (somehow the notion seemed strange, and I could not be certain that I was not delirious) a person who can confess:

> I am a double-Marxist-Freudian-Joycean. My great heroes are the two Marxes — Karl and Groucho — as well as Sigmund Freud and James Joyce. I have developed my own school for sociological investigation which I describe as the Berger "stream of consciousness school of psycho-cultural analysis." A few nasty people have interpreted this to mean that I make my stuff up as I go along and just throw charts and diagrams in to fool sociologists.

"That is, while my focus is frequently a bit more sociological or overtly social scientific than many of the new journalists, and my style is not as jazzy, our concerns are frequently identical — *describing and explicating various aspects of American culture.* Where culture analysis and culture criticism stops and where pop culture and the new journalism begin is beyond me. And, as I said, I don't know where to draw the line between pop culture and the new journalism — except, perhaps at extreme cases."

"Well," said *Arthur Prime*, "I'm not sure what I ought to do. I think I'll stick around for a while!"

I found the thought of having to wander around with not only an alter-ego but an alter-being monstrous, and decided to dispatch him by the best means at my disposal — giving a few lectures that would drive him, as they had driven countless numbers of my students, off. I started with my "Bibliographic Sources Useful for the Study of Contemporary Culture," and noticed he had developed a woeful look and was turning green. I then launched into an analysis of Roland Barthes' semiological work and reviewed his *Mythologies* and *S/Z*, connecting Barthes with the structuralist school and reading several unintelligible passages from Michel Foucault. *Arthur Prime* was trembling, his body racked with nervous twitches and spasms. I finished him off with a lecture on the California state government, the state constitution and related matters.

"You bastard," he shrieked, and there was a sudden poof and whiff — he disappeared in a pale miasmic puff of smoke, the only sign of his existence being a residue of noxious liquids on the floor which smoked and gave off a sulphuric odor, indicating the presence of the diabolical one . . . the supreme alienist. (I was exultant — I was, after all, a *prime mover*.)

III

The new journalism, though often reading like fiction, is not like fiction. It is, or should be, as reliable as most reliable reportage although it seeks a larger truth than is possible through the mere compilation of verifiable facts, the use of direct quotations, and adherence to the rigid organizational style of the older form. The new journalism allows, demands in fact, a more imaginative approach to reporting, and it permits the writer to inject himself into the narrative if he wishes, as many writers do, or to assume the role of a detached observer, as others do, including myself.

I try to follow my subjects unobtrusively while observing them in revealing situations, noting their reactions and the reactions of others to them. I attempt to absorb the whole scene, the dialogue and mood, the tension, drama, conflict, and then I try to write it all from the point of view of the persons I am writing about, even revealing whenever possible what these individuals are *thinking* during those moments that I am describing. This latter insight is not obtainable, of course, without the full cooperation of the subject, but if the writer enjoys the confidence and trust of his subjects, it is possible, through interviews, by asking the right question at the right time, to learn and to report what goes on within other people's minds. (Gay Talese, *Fame and Obscurity*.)

Insights and larger truths! What more could anyone wish? What we must recognize is that frequently large truths emerge from rather trivial and commonplace sources. Look, for example, at the work of Tom Wolfe. He writes about the architecture in Las Vegas, about hot-rod heroes, about clothes — about the culture of the common man. The big difference between Wolfe and the so-called serious scholars is that he is self-consciously a stylist, and tries to give us a sense of the *reality* of what he writes about, rather than just appealing to our intellects and making an argument.

What is this new journalism? In a nutshell, it is interpretative reporting with a bit of pizazz. It uses dialogue, it uses narration, it is stream-of-consciousness reportage, it is stylized and highly descriptive, it deals with the superficial aspects and cosmic significance of all kinds of things we generally don't think twice about, it mixes styles, it has a varied structure of fact and imagination, reportage and "fiction," it has personality and character (as contrasted with the anonymous style of most reporting), it attempts to re-create experience rather than just describe it, but most of all — and of prime importance — it concerns itself with meanings and larger truths.

If you read Wolfe and Talese and others and do not recognize that they are "heavy," to use some street language, you are not giving them enough attention, or are being put off by their style. *They are not solemn, but are extremely serious.* In the popular imagination, we identify or equate seriousness with solemnity, so if a writer comes on with a bit of juice or is playful, we tend to think the less of him for this. Most academics are so ponderously heavy, so puffed-up and self-important, so "deep" and so uptight that they say little for fear of making a slip. It would not be congruent with their god-like images of themselves to make a slip; and so the humanities and social sciences are full of technicians, without imagination, who uncover trivial truths, generally at exorbitant costs. Sometimes it costs $100,000 to reject a null hypothesis or affirm a dull hypothesis.

So when the new journalists come along they face a pervasive and frequently unconscious hostility — from the public, which doesn't trust stylists, and from the intelligensia, which is jealous and envious. A basic error, I believe, has been to dismiss the new journalists as entertainers or something of that sort — as "mere journalists" — and not to recognize the significance of their accomplishments or the importance of their subject matter. The fact of the matter is that a lot of lowbrows are working on highbrow material (and deriving comfort from it because they are then, by definition, doing "important" work), and a lot of highbrows are working on lowbrow material. And if something is entertaining it doesn't mean that it must be wrong or superficial.

For example, one of the most avant-garde institutes of the University of Paris, the Center for the Study of Sociology, Anthropology and Semiotics (which used to be the Center for the Study of Mass Communications) is a collection of people who are interested in many subjects which involve popular culture. The French and Italian semioticians have written about many of the subjects the new journalists have written about, though from a different point of view. But like the new journalists, semioticians are also interested in "large truths." My point is, then, that both are mining the same territory and working toward the same ends, though with different methods. If a semiotician like Roland Barthes writes about wrestling or soap or steak and *frits* for a newspaper like *Combat*, is that "mere" journalism? Is Barthes a kind of new journalist? Is he a pop culturist?

My answer is yes! Though he is more than a journalist and more than a pop culturist — just as I am more than both, though at times perhaps neither. Aren't we all?

IV

"Guru," asked the acolyte, "is your style reflective of your subject?" He had that serious look that all students in communications have, confident in their belief that they are zeroing in on the infinite.

I paused to consider my reply.

"Not necessarily," I said, "for that would be falling victim to the fallacy of imitative form. I have always sought to bring order to chaos, to find meaning where there seemed nothing, to find connections where there seemed only to be randomness and confusion. Untimately I hope to achieve a grand synthesis in which I will show that there are codes permeating our culture and structuring our perceptions and actions.

"For the moment, however, I eschew theories of the high as well as middle range, and concentrate upon specific phenomena — relating them, of course, as best I can, to larger truths. Recall that I was the first to explain that the McDonald's hamburger chain is an evangelical religion, and the first to enunciate the notion of *Hambourgeoisement*. Remember how I showed that white bread is anti-ideological, in keeping with the American political sensibility. Don't forget that I identified the sexual identity of household appliances and explained that baseball is a kind of sexual initiation rite. Keep in mind that I was the first to discern that America was undergoing a process of *motelization*, which refers to the industrialization of the household and destruction of the family unit, and that I enunciated the *Berger Hypottythesis*, which argues that the battle of the budget is connected to the toilet training of our congressmen and senators.

"And do not lose sight of my discovery of the *significant he* in the English language (Hebrew instead of Shebrew, Hedonism instead of Shedonism) which has been so instrumental in subjugating the female psyche. (Even our way of analyzing language, Se*man*tics, is a case in point.) And it was I who explained that *Metrecal* is really a modern manifestation of the infant's formula and was related to our desire for absolute love.

"But in all of this," I continued, "and in my recent work on comics and television, I never lost sight of the fact that my mission was to explicate the hidden meaning of significant trivia, to show the importance oï the ordinary."

V

Videmus nunc per speculum in aenigmate, tunc autem facie ad faciem. [St. Paul]

And you all remember, of course, what St. Irenaeus said:

Nihil vacuum neque sine signo apud Dieuem.

VI

"For now we see through a glass darkly; but then face to face," said St. Paul; "In God nothing is empty of sense," said St. Irenaeus. I got these phrases from Huizinga's *Waning of the Middle Ages*, a classic study of "the forms of life, thought and art in France and the Netherlands in the dawn of the Renaissance." I will conclude this section with a statement by Huizinga that is relevant to our concerns:

> The specific forms of the thought of an epoch should not only be studied as they reveal themselves in theological and philosophic speculations, or in the conceptions of creeds, but also as they ap-

pear in practical wisdom and everyday life. *We may even say that the true character of the spirit of an age is better revealed in its mode of regarding and expressing trivial and commonplace things than in the high manifestations of philosophy and science.* For all scholarly speculation, at least in Europe, is affiliated in a very complicated way to Greek, Hebrew, even Babylonian and Egyptian origins, whereas in everyday life the spirit of a race or of an epoch expresses itself naively and spontaneously. [My italics.]

There are many rooms in the Lord's mansion and space enough for sociologists, anthropologists, pop culturists, new journalists — and everyone else. Sometimes, of course, all of the above exist in one person, in people who may also be "unclassifiable images," like myself. The important thing is to get on with understanding the world, with explaining everyday life, with coming to grips with the meaning of events and artifacts and the significant works of popular art, rather than sitting back and plotting the perfect sociology (which is as absurd as plotting the perfect murder, and sounds just as sickening); it is more important that we try to understand, and change, the world. *Praxis* makes perfect, in every sense of the term.

VII

What's this?
Berger split into twain?
Are both selves
Sharing one brain?
I hated him whole . . .
Now with his double role
I think I shall go
Quite insane.

What's this?
Berger split in two parts?
Two persons —
Two heads and two hearts . . .

Two brains or just one?
Quite probably none.
Just right for
A Doctor of Arts.

So it's Arthur
And Now *Arthur Prime*
(He'll do anything
For a good rhyme)
I'm down on my knees
Asking God, "if you please . . .
Don't let him turn . . .
Into threes!"

Popular Culture for Pleasure and Profit

AN INTRODUCTION IN WHICH THE AUTHOR
EXPLAINS THAT HE IS POPULAR CULTURE

A number of years ago a friend told me something that has been most instrumental in my thinking. "When we are young," he said, "we all have some larger purpose, some great thing we hope to do. But what happens is that we find any number of things occur which interrupt our pursuit of this goal and before we know it we are old and we find that our life has been the interruptions and not the grand undertaking we had originally pointed ourselves towards."

For most people, who lead lives of "quiet desperation," life is the *interruptions*, the momentary pleasures, the lost moments — and not any kind of grand undertaking. And what of all those who never even had a larger purpose, who never thought much about doing anything more than making money and having a good time? And what about those who are disciplined? What about writers and scholars and statesmen? What about athletes? What about concert pianists? Even people with "culture" and people who have accomplished many things, people who have made fortunes and sat with kings — they still have to go to the bathroom, and quite likely they wonder, from time to time, what they'll be having for dinner on any given evening.

The fact of the matter is that we are all ensconced in mundane matters, in trivial concerns, in petty considerations. It is only that some people rise beyond the everyday, tear themselves away — for a time — from interruptions and realize the goals they sought, or in some situations, transcend even their highest aspirations. But it is hard to break loose from the tyranny of everyday life.

In my own particular case this is quite evident. It so happens that I have been keeping a journal since 1954, and have written nearly thirty 300-page volumes of notes, impressions, and trivia. I do a great deal of my thinking "in" the journal: I list things I have to do, write people's names and addresses, draw pictures of things I've bought or hope to buy, draw cartoons, etc.

If you were to look at the journals you would probably say, "My God, the guy has hardly had an idea in his life! All he does is write about trivial things. What junk!" Of course! That's what life is, for the most part. My life is a series of groceries bought at the supermarket, movies I've been to, minor repairs around the house, departmental meetings, with an occasional aside to wonder about something that has struck my attention.

Thus I "am" popular culture — and so are you! I hope that I am a bit more than just popular culture, but that is the base upon which any superstructure is built, and my life, like anybody's life, is an admixture of bits and pieces of popular culture and an occasional refinement. Art is frosting upon the stale bread of life.

THE LAST WORD IN THE ANALYSIS OF POPULAR CULTURE — FROM AN UNCLASSIFIABLE IMAGE

The last word in the analysis of popular culture is culture! That is what it is all about. But what is *culture*? asked Pilate, smiling. There are so many different definitions of culture that it is easy to become confused. Or course we are using the term "culture" in its anthropological sense and not concerning ourselves with aesthetics. Literary scholars and others have a different understanding of the term — they think of it as involving literary and artistic productions which appeal only to sophisticated and trained sensibilities.

The anthropological definition of culture which we will be using is taken from Henry Pratt Fairchild's *Dictionary of Sociology and Related Sciences* (Your College Course At a Glance):

> A collective name for all behavior patterns socially acquired and transmitted by means of symbols; hence a name for all the distinctive achievements of human groups, including not only such items as language, tool-making, industry, art, science, law, government, morals and religion, but also the material instruments or artifacts in which cultural achievements are embodied and by which intellectual cultural features are given practical effect, such as buildings, tools, machines, communication devices, art objects, etc. . . . As culture is transmitted by processes of teaching and learning, whether formal or informal, by what is called "inter-learning," the essential part of culture is to be found in the patterns embodied in the social traditions of the group, that is, the knowledge, ideas, beliefs, values, standards and sentiments prevalent in the group.[1]

According to this definition *everybody* has culture; indeed, to be human is to become, in the anthropological sense of the term, cultured. And if we want to know "about man" we must investigate his everyday activities as well as his intellectual, artistic and philosophical creations.

"No man," it has been said, "is great to his butler." This is because when we get to know someone on a personal level and become aware of his little quirks, his deficiencies, etc., the illusion of greatness is shattered — and we see him for what he is, a person, like anyone else in more ways generally than he is unlike anyone else, who, like all of us, is probably more to be pitied than condemned. Could it be that one reason people have ignored popular culture is that it takes man off his pedestal and smashes all kinds of romantic notions we have about ourselves?

There are a number of other reasons why popular culture has been ignored. Many of its critics argue that it contains little of significance and that it is a waste of time to take it seriously. Proponents of the "popular culture as junk" position claim that it is, for the most part, mechanical, mass-produced, subliterary "schlock," manufactured to please the lowest common denominator.

This view reflects an elitist bias which pervades the academic world, and perhaps society in general. We are all so thirsty for "the best that has been thought and said" that we forget about the everyday and routine aspects of our own lives and about the culture of the common man. In doing so we deny ourselves a perspective on our own lives and on society that might act as a kind of corrective to the distortions we get by limiting ourselves to the view from on high.

We are like Antaeus . . . . If we don't touch the ground we become weak. If we don't recognize the source of our strength and our ties to everyday life we can fly off on all kinds of flights of fancy and lose touch with reality. I'm not arguing against studying "high" culture; I'm just suggesting that popular culture is a legitimate field of inquiry and that we neglect it at our peril.

As a matter of fact, a great deal of our so-called "high" culture is permeated by "low" culture. Marshall McLuhan points out that Joyce was steeped in "lowbrow" culture and used it in writing *Ulysses*: "To write his epic of the modern Ulysses he studied all his life the ads, the comics, the pulps, and popular speech."[2] He also suggests that Little Orphan Annie deals with themes which many "serious" American writers have neglected:

In her isolation and feminine "helplessness" Harold Gray has portrayed for millions of readers the central success drama of America — that of the young, committed to the rejection of parents, that they may justify both the parents and themselves.

Curiously, it is not a theme that "serious" writers have chosen to exploit since Mark Twain. We have here just one instance of popular entertainment keeping in play a major psychological tension in America to which the sophisticated writers are often blind.[3]

I would also claim that popular culture, mass culture, whatever you wish to call it, has — in certain cases — literary, artistic, and philosophical merit as well as sociological significance in its own right.

It is as difficult to define popular culture as it is to define culture, per se. Probably it is easier to characterize pop culture and say that it involves the entertainments and activities of the common man, of the populace in general. Thus a pop culturist would study such things as comic strips and comic books, advertisements, joke cycles, fads, folklore of all sorts, radio and television programs, the cinema, fashions, foods, popular fiction, sports, and all of what Malinowski called the "imponderabilia" of everyday life. It is all that is *not* elite culture — and yet, since much of elite culture becomes, at time, popular culture, it cannot completely exclude elite culture.

Popular culturists lack an academic identity. (Someone once described me as an unclassifiable image.) You have to be a generalist and interdisciplinarian to be a good pop culturist and it is not easy work, by any means. But pop culturists have the most fun!

> *Question:*   Aren't you really a cultural anthropologist?
> *Answer:*   Isn't everyone?

A CAUTIONARY NOTE FROM A CRITIC ON CRITICISM, WITH A FEW THEORETICAL CONSIDERATIONS THROWN IN

The critic of popular culture has the task of *analyzing, interpreting,* and *evaluating* whatever it is he is interested in. Since much of popular culture has an artistic or aesthetic component (no matter how dreadful this may be), it is important that we do not look upon popular culture and popular art as merely documents to be mined for incidences of violence, proportions of this or that, etc. We must take into account the conventions of each popular art (and perhaps the popular arts in general) and other aesthetic considerations. For example, in many cases form has a "content" of its own, and to neglect formal and structural matters is simple-minded.

The problem with most of the work done in popular culture is that the sociologists have neglected aesthetic considerations and the literary scholars have neglected sociological considerations. Popular culture has been an easy target or people with any one of a number of biases.

It may very well be that second-rate movies and other manifestations of mediocrity and bad taste have a great deal to tell us about our society. As Huizinga said in *Waning of the Middle Ages*: "We may even say that the true character of the spirit of an age is better revealed in its mode of regarding and expressing trivial and commonplace things than in the high manifestations of philosophy and science."[5] We cannot burn with hard, gem-like flames all the time and the average man is just that — average. (Actually, fifty percent of the population is above average and fifty percent is below average, so there may not be an "average" man or woman.) It follows then that, at times, it pay to lower our gaze and, taking a moment to tear our eyes away from celestial visions and delights, examine our feet to see whether they are stuck in the mud?

Now it may be that the critic of popular culture will conclude that it is, for the most part, a destructive force — that it stimulates aggression, despair, self-hatred, consumer-lust, or any one of a thousand other evil things. In such cases it is the task of the pop culturist to prove his charge, as best he can. What is important is that we should not operate on too high a level of abstraction and just talk about popular culture and society. We must get down to concrete instances, to specifics; otherwise we are not critics (as I interpret the term) but philosophers of one sort or another. There is nothing wrong with being a media *guru*, but there is a lot of spade work to be done yet in the trenches.

We know that popular culture is a socializing agent. In *Television and Growing Up: The Impact of Televised Violence*, the Surgeon General's Scientific Advisory Committee on Television and Social Behavior, it was reported that: "Commercial television in the United States has not primarily attempted to be a teaching agent; its self-chosen primary role has been to entertain. Entertainment, however — whether via television or not — may unobtrusively convey ideas, information, sentiments, and values to the members of a society."[6] The same report stated: "Varieties of television fare can structure the audience member's relationship to reality. To varying extents and in various ways they can engage conscience, modify or mobilize opinion, and challenge or confirm beliefs."[7] The same applies to all forms of popular culture. What is important is that we provide examples of all this and show how people are affected by popular culture.

There are four focal points to which we can direct our attention, that for the sake of alliteration I call: *America*, the work of *Art*, the *Author*, and *Audience*.

Our basic concern should be the work of Art and the way it relates to (mediates between) American society and the Audience, that is, the

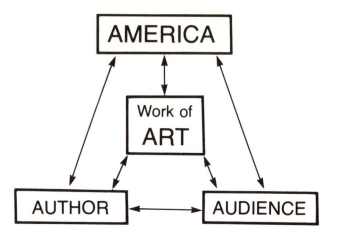

Focal Points in Analysis of Popular Culture

general public. The relationships are very complex. When I talk about a work of Art, please remember that I might be talking about a film, a detective novel or a McDonald's hamburger.

Now the way we deal with the various considerations or focal-points I have just mentioned depends, to a large degree, upon the "theory of art" we hold. In many cases we are not aware or conscious that we hold a "theory of art," but we must if we have given any thought to art and culture and things of that nature. I have developed an acronym for the theories of art: POEM, which stands for the *Pragmatic, Objective, Emotive*, and *Mimetic* theories of art.

These theories are briefly explained in the folllowing chart:

THEORIES OF ART

Pragmatic: art does a job — teaches, propagandizes, etc.

Objective: art projects its own reality, own world.

Emotive: art gives kicks, creates an emotional response.

Mimetic: art imitates, reflects, mirrors reality.

It is obvious that there is a contradiction between the pragmatic and emotive, and the objective and mimetic theories of art. A person who values the arts because of the emotional "kicks" he gets from them will not respond to something the way a pragmatist does, who thinks art should teach or do some kind of job. And a person who values the arts for the world they project (the lamp) will not be too interested in the notion that the arts are most valuable because they reflect reality (the mirror).

There are no answers to these problems, but it is important that you recognize that there are different ways of valuing the arts and popular culture before you start analyzing either. It is obvious that people who spend time examining and analyzing pop culture critically assume that it "mirrors" or "reflects" (in certain ways) reality, but it is not quite that simple. There is also the matter of pop culture's various functions — its pragmatic aspects — and it may very well be that the way pop culture functions in society has something to do with the emotive and projective aspects of a given work of pop culture.

A MODEST PARADIGM IS OFFERED THAT HAS UNIVERSAL IMPLICATIONS — FOR THOSE WHO CAN UNDERSTAND IT

The paradigm that follows represents an attempt I have made to tie together as many aspects and threads which involve a given act, popular culture, myths, media, and whatever else you will, as I can. There are a number of places one can "start" at in this paradigm, but probably the best place is in the central block in which a person "acts."

This act may be, and probably will be, something that we would call "pop culture." It could be something like mowing a lawn, taking a ride at an amusement park, barbequing a steak, or watching a television program. This act, as I see things (and have shown in my paradigm), is part of a stream of acts that involve all kinds of other acts; it is part of a complex web of stimuli, responses, impulses, unconscious imperatives, rational decisions, which are connected, in various ways, to legends, myths, works of high and popular culture, artifacts, and so forth.

All the material below the two highest levels — the historical and sociological — involves a specific person and the whole complex world of myth and art and experience that is "behind" any given act. What I call "sociological" refers to the various social sciences that look for patterns in acts or study classes of acts, for one reason or another. I have arbitrarily, put history on the top of the heap as that discipline which studies changes and continuities in time and which tries to make sense of everything beneath it in the paradigm.

Paradigms are, of course, artificial constructions and subject to all kinds of difficulties. My main purpose in constructing my paradigm is to suggest that there are many different complex relationships that must be considered in analyzing an act or example of popular culture. We find

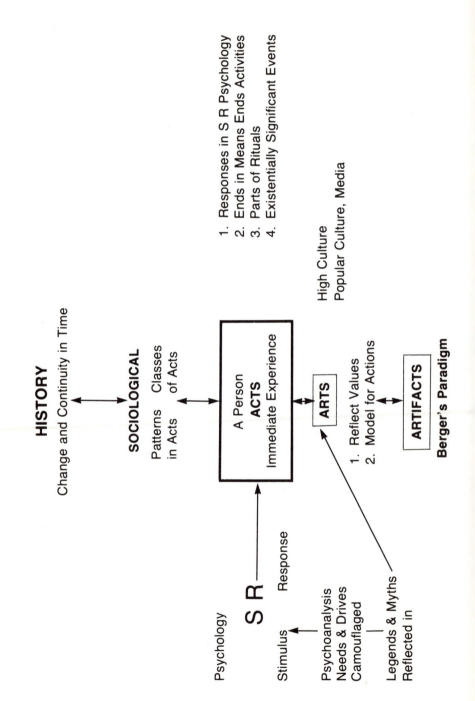

HISTORY
Change and Continuity in Time

SOCIOLOGICAL
Patterns   Classes
in Acts   of Acts

A Person
ACTS
Immediate Experience

1. Responses in S R Psychology
2. Ends in Means Ends Activities
3. Parts of Rituals
4. Existentially Significant Events

High Culture
Popular Culture, Media

ARTS
1. Reflect Values
2. Model for Actions

ARTIFACTS
Berger's Paradigm

Psychology

S R

Stimulus   Response

Psychoanalysis
Needs & Drives
Camouflaged

Legends & Myths
Reflected in

ourselves with a paradox as far as pop culture analysis is concerned: the simpler anything is, the more difficult it is to explain. It is not too much of a job to find significance in a classic work of literature or piece of art; but to find the significance in a piece of junk, even to understand why a bad work of pop culture or "high" literature is bad — that takes some doing!

The paradigm works, as I said, from the center out and focuses upon a person acting, a person doing something specific. The paradigm helps tie this act to the world at large and shows how a given act can be connected to any number of aspects (depending upon your knowledge and imagination) of the world around us.

There is, however another way of operating — and that is operating at a higher or more impersonal level of abstraction. In this procedure we take a myth and show how it has manifested itself, in general, on the social scene. To make this clearer, I have developed a "Myth Model" which follows:

THE MYTH MODEL

1. The Myth
2. Historical Acts
3. High Culture
4. Popular Culture
5. Everyday life

When we use the myth model we take some myth and "run it through" the model, seeing how it has affected or "informed" different aspects of our culture and society. For example, I have (elsewhere) taken the myth of natural paradise and discussed it in terms of its impact upon American history, and its various manifestations in American literature and popular culture as well as "everyday life."[8] It can be found in the movement of the Puritans to America, in the frontier, in our utopian communities, in our notion of American as a "natural paradise" full of American Adams, in Westerns, Disneyland, science fiction, suburbs, nature foods, nudist colonies, etc., etc.

I have been influenced in my thinking about myth by the work of Mircea Eliade, who said in *Myths, Dreams and Mysteries:* "Certain mythical themes still survive in modern societies, but are not readily recognizable since they have undergone a long process of laicization."[9] His book *The Sacred and the Profane* deals with myth on a very high level of abstraction, and though it is not particularly focused upon American culture (or any culture) much of what he says can be applied here.

It may be best to think of our culture and society as something like an onion, and as we peel away the outer layers, we find, ultimately, a core of myth that has shaped everything else. It may be that there is a lot of John Wesley in our myth, which would mean that in addition to method there is also Methodism to our madness? (I wonder what would happen if we were to do our onion peeling with the beat generation?)

Onion Metaphor of Culture and Society

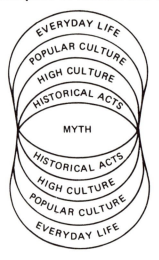

Now that we are in possession of the paradigm, myth model, and onion "metaphor," we are equipped with a considerable number of instruments with which to probe our culture. It is also necessary to have a degree of familiarity with certain disciplines and areas, such as psychoanalysis, sociology, anthropology, literary criticism, etc. (The following is adapted from my essay "The Poop on Pop" in my *Pop Culture*.) We must consider the following questions:

Historical Analysis: When did whatever it is you are investigating get started? Is it different now from the way it used to be? If so, why? If not, why not? When was it popular? Was it popular at a particular time for a particular reason? What does it tell us about the period in which it was popular?

Comparative Analysis: Is the same thing done the same way elsewhere? Do different cultures or countries have variations that are interesting? Can we get any statistical information that might be of value?

Psychoanalytical Investigation: Does whatever it is you are studying take care of certain needs we all have? Does it help us deal with anxiety or frustration or anger? Does it reassure us? Calm us? Excite us? What are its functions as far as our "unconscious" is concerned?

Sociological Analysis: What class levels are appealed to? Does your subject have a racial or ethnic slant to it? Does it appeal to some groups (whether they be of a class, religious, racial, geographic or other nature) and not others? Does it have any political significance to it?

Myth-Symbol-Ritual Analysis: Can your subject be related in any way to important myths which have either universal or particular (to a country or group) significance? Does it have a symbolic dimension to it which makes it interesting? Can your subject be looked upon as a kind of (or part of a) ritual?

Content Analysis: How often (many times per minute, page, episode) is a given kind of behavior (violence, stereotyping of people) observed? What are the basic ideas, values, images and beliefs that are to be found in some publication or program — generally speaking, which is part of a series. What patterns emerge?

Semiotic/Structuralist Analysis: If you think of whatever it is you are examining as a sign or, if it is complex, as a system of signs, what do you find? What are the interesting internal relationships found in your topic? Can your subject be looked at as if it were a system in which certain elements are found in certain patterns? And what set of polar oppositions can be found in your subject which generates meaning?

These questions indicate that the basic function of the pop culturist is to analyze and explicate things, to deal with the social, political, and psychological significance of pop culture and not to deal with pop culture only from a historical point of view. Pop culture can be used to shed light on history, but a history of pop culture, which focuses on when this or that happened and vaguely upon what pop culture "reveals" about society, is not, to my way of thinking, terribly important.

ENTER THE SECRET AGENT:
CONFESSION OF A COUNTERCULTURE SPY

A number of years ago I had an embosser made for myself which reads: Arthur Asa Berger, Writer, Artist, Secret Agent. I stamp it on most of the letters I send to friends and everyone finds it most amusing. Somehow the notion that a professor could be a secret agent is quite crazy; it is also absurd for secret agents to advertise themselves as such.

I have over the years developed the drawing which follows — a symbolization of the *essence* of secret agentry: a man (myself), his face wrapped in shadows, in a slouch hat and raincoat, poised with a revolver — at the ready! This imagined manifestation of myself is as far removed as possible from my day-to-day activities, which involve lecturing, grading term papers, going to department meetings, and that sort of thing.

And yet... and yet, *I really am a secret agent!* Not the kind of secret agent who works for governments and steals plans for bombs and missiles. I am a self-employed secret agent — who searches, relentlessly, for hidden meanings and latent functions, for unconscious imperatives and unrecognized *relationships.* I get my kicks from my discoveries, and as I work, I like to think that like all secret agents I shake the very foundations of society. For if society maintains itself on the basis of the unrecognized (latent) functions of the various activities people engage in, when I point out these latent functions I make them recognizable (manifest) and as I do so, the equilibrium in society is disturbed. The paradox of sociological knowledge, as someone once explained it to me, is that the more we know, the worse off we are, if in fact it is the latent functions of our activities that maintain society. Thus I am a secret agent who discovers secrets and broadcasts them (when I can get someone to publish my work) to the world.

It is all very comic and mad, but in a world that someone, I believe it was Santayana, once described as "an equilbrium of idiocies," a secret agent here and there may tip the balance. And what, I ask you, if I were really a secret agent? My idiocies might make all the difference! (Idiocy, by the way, come from idios — or private. An idiot is one who leads a private life.) The function of my secret agentry is to expose the hidden, or in some cases private, significance of things. A correspondence can be made between psychological and sociological interest in hidden or covert matters:

FUNCTIONS AND CONSCIOUSNESS

Psychology	*Sociology*
the unconscious	latent functions
the conscious	manifest functions
the individual	society (institutions)

The basic question, which decides where on the chart you operate, is whether you are concerned with the psyche or with society, though in many cases you will be interested in both.

Of course, as a secret agent, I face many problems. How do I know I haven't been lied to? How do I know I haven't read "too much" into things? How do I know that my analyses are not too subjective? partial? superficial? too profound? How can I be sure that my suspicions about the meaning of things to people's psyches are correct? How can I be sure that what I'm interested in is not atypical and unusual? How can I be sure that my secrets are worth anything?

The answer is that I can't. All I can do is build a case which will convince a reasonable person that my secrets are valuable and worth something. I don't claim infallibility. I am a secret agent and not the Pope!

One question: is an unmarried female spy a spynster?

Another question: can bookkeepers be members of the counterculture?

A CONCLUSION IN WHICH A MAN WITHOUT IDEAS OFFERS A NUMBER OF THEM TO THINK ABOUT.

A. Do Freudians, with their passion for the Oedipus complex, have a natural affinity for *Pop* Culture? Do we think of the highway patrol, and police in general, as "father figures" who punish us for not playing with our toys the right way?

B. Is the free-floating hostility that permeates our society a function of our individualism? What relation exists between this hostility and our greed for event-participation? Is it because we feel we are nobodies that we want to take part, even if as spectators, in "history"?

C. As one ascetic said to another, "That's okay, but just don't let *id* happen again."

D. Is romantic love in America connected with our individualism? After all, it is one of the few areas in which initiative counts for the average person, and his power to "thrill" is one of the few he still retains — if, indeed, he does retain it?

E. Speaking of the tape recorder, is there any relationship between dictating and dictators?

F. Is yoghurt the epitome of homogenized mass culture?

G. Is there a difference between a *lowest* common denominator and a *largest* common denominator?

H. Clare Booth/Was Luce/But Martin/Was Luther.
   Aga/Khan/But Immanuel/Kant.

I. What is the relation that exists between our economic system and our cultural system? Is there such a thing as a "culture of capitalism"? Is that what explains tendencies in our culture towards massification, commercialization, vicariousness, consumer-lust and subjectivism? Does praxis make perfect?

J. Is it the genius of fashion that we are condemned if we do *not* act "like everyone else does"?

K. All good things come to those Kuwait!

L. Is there an inverse relation between the power of a car's engine and the sense of "self" of the owner? Do muscle cars exist for men who secretly think of themselves as weaklings?

M. Are politicians who prate about balancing the budget and fiscal conservatism "anal erotics" who have transferred their obsession with their stools to the national budget? (This is known as the Berger Hypottythesis.)

N. Do Americans have a true sense of tragedy, or do we substitute irony for tragedy here? An egalitarian society is not so much concerned with the fall of "great" men as with men making mistakes which are their undoing. Are we our own worst enemies?

O. Why is popular culture so unpopular?

NOTES

1. Henry Pratt Fairchild, *Dictionary of Sociology and Related Sciences,* (Totowa, N.J.: Littlefield, Adams & Co., 1967), p. 80.
2. Marshall McLuhan, *The Mechanical Bride* (New York: Vanguard Press, 1951), p. 59.
3. Ibid., p. 66
4. Arthur Berger, "Pop Culture: The Secret Significance of the Commonplace," *San Francisco Chronicle, This World* magazine, Jan. 21, 1973. (This article is about my book, *Pop Culture,* Dayton, Ohio: Pflaum/Standard, 1973.)
5. J. Huizinga, *The Waning of the Middle Ages* (New York: Anchor), p. 225.
6. Surgeon General's Scientific Advisory Committee on Television and Social Behavior, *Television and Growing Up: The Impact of Televised Violence,* p. 39.
7. Ibid., pp. 42, 43.
8. For a more complete discussion of the myth model and the myth of paradise see "Popular Culture and Heroes: There's Myth as Well as Method Behind Our Madness" in my *About Man: An Introduction to Anthropology* (Pflaum/Standard, 1974).
9. Mircea Eliade, *Myths, Dreams and Mysteries* (New York: Harper & Row, 1967), p. 28.

Discovering Pop Culture

Has it been a mere five years since the Popular Culture Association held its first meeting? Was it only in 1971 that a group of scholars, students, and fellow travelers "working" the popular culture vein gathered and created an organization and, consequently, an identity for themselves? The time has raced by quickly and, in that brief span, a remarkable development has taken place. For popular culture is now a "major" minor area in the American educational landscape, and academics at all levels are beginning to process their environment and examine the culture in which they find themselves.

Of course, there are many people in the traditional disciplines who feel that it is as much a waste of time to study popular culture as to enjoy or "consume" it, but despite protestations from elitists on the one hand, and troglodytes on the other, the beat goes on. An estimated 600 of the faithful (the number, given to me by Ray Browne, who organized the conference, may have been a bit optimistic) gathered at the Chase-Park Plaza Hotel in St. Louis to give papers, argue about what popular culture is and isn't, see old friends, look for jobs that don't exist (to any significant degree), and carry on the way academics do at all conventions.

But what is popular culture, you may ask? Would that I or anyone else could really tell you. Generally speaking, when we talk about popular culture we define it as involving widely disseminated and broadly appealing art forms such as westerns, detective stories, commercials, space operas, soap operas, situation comedies, pulp literature of all persuasions, fast foods, commonplace objects or so-called material culture, plus a great deal that we do on a routine day-to-day basis. The popular arts are distributed by the familiar media: print, radio, television, records, and the movies, but we may also want to consider modes of transmission such as franchises and supermarkets as kinds of media.

While everyone would probably agree that comic strips and comic books, advertisements, rock music, sports, and situation comedies are popular culture, there are problems when we leave obvious kinds of popular culture and move to fringe areas and borderline situations. Some people see folk art as separate from popular culture and others don't know where to draw the line between popular culture and elite art—art that requires a trained sensibility and a certain amount of "sophistication" to appreciate. But, to cite a problem—if Hamlet is broadcast on television and 30 million people see it, is it popular culture or elite culture? And if something is popular, does it mean it is automatically bad? (Conversely, if something is unpopular, does it mean it is automatically good?) The old saw that popular culture *must* be junk because it *must* appeal to the mythical "lowest common denominator" doesn't seem very persuasive now. Why not the *largest* common denominator?

And what was going on in St. Louis in the cavernous and decaying old monolith where the flock had gathered together? A list of some of the papers read is most instructive and can be found below.

To the uninitiated, academic conventions have a bizarre and unworldly character. The amount of effort and energy devoted to obscure and frequently irrelevant pursuits seems almost obscene in a world plagued with moral degeneracy and spiritual paralysis. And yet, so we are told—and so academicians are wont to believe—it is by piling paper upon paper that knowledge progresses, for it is the minutiae that make possible the quantum leaps. One can only hope that this is so and that the thousands and hundreds of thousands of hours spent investigating American-Turkish diplomacy from 1895-1900 or the courting behavior of Chinese adolescents is leading us toward a better and more humane society.

Thus, if we were to peek into the rooms at the Chase-Park Plaza, we might find papers being offered on "Sexual Hang-ups and the American Gangster" or "The Machine as a Sexual Object" or "J. Edgar Hoover and the Detective Hero" or "Religion and Social Hygiene in *The Reader's Digest*." You might prefer "Stereotypes in Chicano Cuisine" or "Swinging and Swapping: Popular Views of Organized Adultery" or perhaps "Sex-Role Exchange and Other Subliminal Fantasies in Bram Stoker's *Dracula*." Those with more down-to-earth interests might have been intrigued by papers on "Schlitz Saloon Architecture in Turn-of-the-Century Chicago" or "Observations of Pacific Northwest Barn Types."

Other intriguing titles were "Neon As Sign Art Form," "Knuckle Down: Anyone for Marbles?" "Doubling Your Health: The Chewing Gum Industry," "Play and Sports in Black Literature," and "The Image of the Religious in Contemporary Pornography." In short, there was a dazzling variety of subjects under analysis—foods, fads, entertainments, preoccupations, leisure-time activities—and what was most remarkable was that this seemingly esoteric list of topics and titles was, in truth, centered upon the banalities of our everyday life. What seems so remarkable is that, at long last, we are begining to take an interest in our routine activities and entertainments, for that is what popular culture is, in part—an investigation of everyday life and the culture of the common man. Were the same thing to be done for a tribe of preliterate aborigines in some far-off land, it wouldn't raise an academic eyebrow. The food preferences, myths, rituals, and other imponderabilia of everyday life are the subject matter of anthropologists and other kinds of scholars. Yet to investigate the same phenomena in our own societies seems quite incredible.

What is popular culture about? It is about humankind, about our culture. And what is it that everyone was talking about in St. Louis? Essentially a combination of the *aesthetic significance of "culture"* and the *anthropological meaning of "culture,"* which involves behavior patterns and belief systems that are socially acquired and symbolically transmitted. How to reconcile the two points of view is a continuing problem for pop culturists.

* * *

Stately, thin, John G. Cawelti, professor of humanities at the University of Chicago and president of the Popular Culture Association, came from the stairhead of the Chase-Park Plaza with that look of self-assurance that characterizes all national presidents of learned societies with another year to go in the saddle. He had changed remarkably. Gone was the Iowa crew cut; in its stead, a head of hair of leonine proportions cascaded about him. His beard was now long and fluffy, patriarchal, almost—the beard of a man every inch a president. He was dressed informally, parading his might and power in his plaid shirt, casual slacks, and shoes.

Presidents need not impress anyone and so they emphasize this by seeming utterly irrelevant and harmless. His relaxed gait and ease were symbols of his security, a security bred not only by his office but by his position as one of the leading "theorists" of the popular culture movement. He had two guns in his armory; for many men are presidents and not theorists and some are theorists and not presidents, but few are both presidents *and* theorists. Of course, all theorists will tell you, if you ask them, that all organizations should be led by theorists—and an organization as inchoate and bizarre as the Popular Culture Association, a strange concatenation of scholars from all kinds of disciplines, a mixed-up organization such as this certainly needed a theorist at its helm. Cawelti is kind and gentle, the way men of genuine achievement often are. Puffed-up arrogant people are seldom presidents of national associations.

His *Six-Gun Mystique* has been hailed as a minor literary classic by many popular culturists, although others claim it is basically synthetic, merely weaves together a number of strands from here and there and is not "original." Even if this complaint were true, we must ask—how many theories are original? How much of anything is original? To pop culturists, originality (whatever that is) is not necessarily the highest virtue.

All presidents and theorists are used to complaints. You can't please everyone, so you might as well please yourself, if you can get away with it. In St. Louis, there was so much being said about so many things that, in truth, everyone was happy to have him there for they could derive a bit of comfort from the belief that somehow, out of it all, something grand and remarkable, a theory that unified all the seemingly random exploration, would emerge. It was known that Cawelti would be bringing forth a book on formulas, a book that would do what all theories do—call attention to themselves as seemingly the only possible explanation for everything—at that time.

Einstein had uttered $E = MC^2$ and the universe shook.

What would John Cawelti say? And what would happen?

The last I saw him he was telling a marvelous joke about the Pope and the chief rabbi of Rome, which involved his making elaborate gestures and motions. It was slightly mad, but presidents of mad organizations are given a great deal of latitude by their followers. In the background lurked the gray eminence Ray B. Browne, secretary-treasurer of the association and the real power in the organization. The Popular Culture Association may have a president who is a theoretician and can speak in formulas, but it is very much, to this moment, a Brownean movement.

* * *

As with all movements with vitality and life, the popular culture movement is in the process of change and transition. Born of a dalliance between Clio the Muse and a depraved English professor or two, popular culture is a "spiritual orphan" amongst the established disciplines. It lacks their "dignity" and status. Originally, pop culture was connected with American studies, itself a half-breed in academia, and it still maintains a tenuous connection (Tenuous, anyone?). But unlike American studies, which has become rather servile and dull in its quest for respectability (we might say it is prostituting itself for the bitch-goddess Status), pop culture revels in its obtuseness and glories in its ignominiousness.

Let the stuffed shirts in the so-called respectable disciplines carry on—now that students aren't forced into their courses, many of the grandees in the traditional subject areas are being reduced to talking to themselves and a handful of disciples. I don't begrudge people in the disciplines their bowl of pottage (soups—a good pop culture subject) but I do resent their generally smug and supercilious attitude about what is proper scholarship. Pop culture, they tell us, is good "fun" (which means, automatically, trivial), but it isn't important! Perhaps?

What has happened lately is that a number of people who have been working in mass communications, sociology, English, American studies, and many other areas have suddenly had a shock of recognition. They have discovered that deep down in the jungle they are really pop culturists—and once pop culture became a subject matter, they achieved an identity, even though it may be a rather diffuse one.

Now people in popular culture are beginning to move away from strictly literary, historical, and sociological perspectives. We are beginning to find structuralist and semiotic (the science of signs) approaches, influenced in large part by work done in France and Italy. A Marxist critique of popular culture is emerging and making itself felt more strongly. In the space of just a few years, a dozen or more textbooks have suddenly appeared on the scene and popular culture courses are now taught in high school as well as at higher levels. Folklorists all over are starting to pay attention to the twentieth century and are applying their techniques to urban folklore, which is very close to popular culture as I define it. A Finnish folklorist at the University of Helsinki, Matti Kuusi, calls the union of folklore and pop culture "Poplore," and his students are writing about kiosk (pulp) literature and similar subjects.

The conference began with an address by the distinguished humanist Walter J. Ong, S. J., on African talking drums—slit-gongs. These drums, he said, are an integral part of African popular culture and have a great deal to tell us about oral communication in African culture, and in all cultures, by extension. The conference concluded with sessions on popular culture and literature, leisure time, video, and fittingly, Afro-American popular culture.

There were complaints, as might be expected, about a number of things: the cost of rooms at the hotel, the absence of students (who are no longer provided with housing by the association), the quality of some of the papers and the fact that some of them were read, word by word, instead of delivered. The Popular Culture Association does have its problems, as do all organizations. But the gathering of marginal souls on the academic body politic is on to something important and is having a considerable impact on the scholarly world. It is forcing academics to come to grips with the elitism entrenched in the universities and the irrelevance of much that is done in academia by people pursuing their private passions.

Ray Browne was quoted in an article entitled "Pop Culture: Meaningful or Meatball?" in the *St. Louis Post Dispatch*. "It is a new view of the humanities,'' he said, but I would go further and suggest it is a new view of people in all our dimensions, and as with most new views, it is based upon some very old views.

Not only can it be said, then, that at least in certain ways "Malt does more than Milton can,'' but also that meatballs have meaning and that to understand American culture, one must understand the higher significance of the hamburger and of (to adopt a Marxist stance) the *hambourgeoisement* that is so rampant here. What pop culturists recognize, and the implications of this insight are profound, is that when you can read all things not only in a cathedral or a grain of sand, but also in a meatball, you are on the path toward understanding humanity and society.

The Ugly Ones: Images of Americans in Asia and Elsewhere

America is, it has been suggested, a "self-conscious" society. When we do not mortify ourselves for failing to be perfect—or, at least, not living up to our high expectations for ourselves, we indulge in endless speculation about who we are. Watergate and revelations about hanky-panky in Washington have tended to tarnish our image in one sense, and build it up in another. I don't think we hold such lofty notions about our social and political morality anymore though; ironically, our self-exposures have convinced others that we are highly moral. But we have not solved our identity problem by any means.

An attempt to make some progress in more sharply defining the American image was made recently at a research seminar in popular culture held at the East-West Center in Honolulu. Eight Asian and three American scholars met for the better part of a month and gave reports on research they did on popular images of America in various countries. I was one of the American scholars and the seminar was quite a remarkable experience. It was the first extended encounter I've had with Asian academics and intellectuals and it revealed to me, firsthand, how difficult it is to communicate across cultural borders. Though most of the Asians in the seminar had been to American universities and learned their research methods here, they were all careful about their national identities—and many of them were highly critical of American society and culture.

Images of America in most foreign countries tend to be negative, or at best, ambivalent ones; that should come as no surprise. After all, we are the most powerful and affluent society in the world and many smaller and weaker countries resent and fear us. (The Vietnam war was brought up again and again. It gave us a very negative image.) Some countries, which received foreign aid, didn't think we gave them enough aid or didn't like the strings which were attached to this aid. Other countries

33

were afraid of economic exploitation and a phrase that came up over and over again, "cultural imperialism." It is expensive to produce films and television programs so many countries import American media products. Our films and television shows tend to be dominant in some countries and there is a fear that traditional cultures will be destroyed and that modernization or development will lead to "Americanization"—the worst of all possible fates!

It turns out that most countries are full of Coca-Cola, McDonald's hamburger stands, Kentucky Fried Chicken stores, and so on. American fast foods and popular culture tend to create our images nowadays; in the old days it was G.I. Joe, who liked to fool around, it seems, with the native girls wherever he was. Between our soldiers and our popular culture, we have given many people rather bad images of ourselves. The situation is complicated; everyone recognizes that soldiers (and tourists) do not give the best of impressions. Many of these people in the seminar came from countries which had had experience with Japanese soldiers as well as American ones. Furthermore, people have a tendency to compare our popular culture with their traditional and elite cultures, which always makes us look rather bad.

Some people in other lands don't know that Coca-Cola is an American product! One person asked me whether we had Shakey's pizza in America. (She had never been to the mainland.) We didn't resolve the problem of our so-called cultural imperialism (also known as Coca-Colonization) since it was broght out that imperialism usually involves governmental agencies, etc., and this was just a case of a super-powerful society tending to "dominate" other cultures. There is a problem, but whether it is a matter of imperialism was at issue.

Although everyone spoke English, with varying degrees of proficiency, there were many semantic difficulties. For example, the matter of Americans being *pragmatic* came up one morning. In America the term has positive connotations, suggesting down-to-earthness, practicality, a concern with consequences, etc. But when we asked a Japanese professor how the term was used in Japan, he paused for a moment and said it could be defined there as "tool user." And most of the other participants said the term had very negative connotations in their countries. Pragmatists are seen by most people, if my informants are correct, as unscrupulous, nonidealistic types who will do anything to gain their ends.

A paper by a Japanese professor dealt with Japanese perceptions of American women gained from travelers here in the nineteenth century. These travelers were astounded to see our women on horses, it seems, and thought American society was dominated by women. A paper on Canadian images of Americans suggests that Americanophobia is epidemic amongst our neighbors to the north and that a goodly number of Canadians are suffering from paranoia. We know that sometimes paranoids have fears that are justified, and it may be that Canada has reason to be upset about American economic and cultural dominance (imperialism?).

Short stories in Malaysia tend to be uniformly negative about America, and those in the Philippine mass press have gone from being positive (we were seen as liberators) to being negative (we are seen as exploiters). Pakistani newspaper editorials aren't nice anymore and Indian intellectuals maintain ambivalent positions. An opinion survey of Indians show they like our dynamism and generosity but don't like our violence-filled films and television programs and many other aspects of our society. Only the Iranians, who have bought ten billion dollars worth of military hardware from us (and whose press is government "influenced") were uniformly positive about American culture and society.

One effect of our mass media is that many people are afraid to go to American cities. I detected a note of concern by several of the participants about visiting American cities, and it became a kind of standing joke to tease people about being killed in San Francisco. Our work with images led us to conclude that it is people's images of reality (or perceptions) which shape their attitudes and behavior, so our image as a violence-filled society affects many people. Our Pakistani professor, who planned to visit San Francisco, New York, and Washington, was extremely anxious about his safety and told me he would send me a postcard when he left America so I'd be sure he had survived.

The seminar was led by a Japanese professor, Hidetoshi Kato, who has a part-time appointment at the East-West Center's Communication Institute. He is a distinguished sociologist who has worked with David Riesman and many other important American scholars, and he ran the seminar beautifully. We saw a number of films, did a lot of socializing together, and we all gained a great deal from the experience. Everyone wrote a long paper and revised it during the course of the seminar. We came to no solid conclusions, but that wasn't our goal. After all, if you take people from eight different Asian countries with different backgrounds and different understandings of the word "pragmatism" and many other terms (such as popular culture), you cannot expect to come to any conclusions. But we made a lot of progress, and we learned a good deal about each other's cultures while finding out about the various images of Americans.

For better or worse it is through our popular culture—our fast foods, clothes, films, television shows, etc.—that most poeple know us. Some of us decided that popular culture is, in essence, *the culture of complex societies* and that we are all cultural or pop-cultural anthropologists. American culture is, for most foreign people, American pop culture, and the relationship between the two is hard to figure out! Now that we've all sharpened our analytical tools, we're looking around for other victims for image studies. The popular culture seminar, after three years, has been phased out, but there is a possibility we'll all meet in Japan in two years to participate in a seminar on images of the Japanese. They also seem to have a self-conscious society.

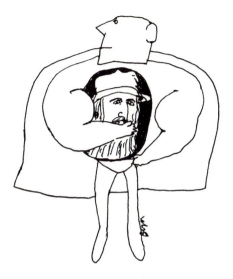

Part 2

Comics

Politics in the Comics

The comic strip is one of those art forms whose very all-pervasiveness and ubiquity blind us to its significance. Certain people, I would call them elitists, suggest that comics and all forms of popular culture are subliterary, mass-produced artifacts which cater to the "lowest common denominator" and that they are of no significance, except as indicators of the power of the mass media to dominate a culture—in the service of bourgeois capitalism, invariably.

I would counter this by suggesting that all forms of expression are connected with ideologies, and the popular culture (and, indeed, elite culture) of nonbourgeois societies is far from innocent and devoid of particular points of view (a charitable term). If the comics and all forms of popular culture do express this so-called "lowest common denominator," that is perfectly fine, because we need to know more about the ideas of the common man—*his* point of view, his notions about the good life and the good society.

The comics can be characterized as having the following attributes: continuing characters, speech in balloons, and a left to right sequence of boxes and balloons. Some comics have continued stories while others, humorous "gag strips," have a new and complete episode each day. Sometimes comic books—actually magazines of comics—carry adventures of various characters and appear regularly, though this innovation is a mere forty years old.

IMPORTANT THEMES IN AMERICAN COMICS

It is difficult to characterize, with any degree of accuracy, American comic strips and comic books. After all, we are dealing with an art form that started in the 1890s and which has flourished since that time. Some of the classic strips are now forty years old and still appearing, and the number of comic books (conventional and underground) is staggering. There is a veritable pantheon of comic characters—heroes, villains, clowns, fools, people, animals, humans, inhumans, robots, machines, spooks, and androids—and with every week that passes, new creations (especially villains to fight with the heroes) find their way into the American "collective imagination."

Nevertheless, American heroes and superheroes do arise out of the American experience and must have meaning to children socialized in America. So despite the diversity of characters in comicdom, there are some things they tend to have in common. In my book, *The Comic-Stripped American,* I detected several themes which are of interest to us here: first, the notion that Americans are "spiritual orphans"; and second, a fundamental anti-authoritarianism, balanced in part by some characters who had great reverence for authority.

I discerned these themes after I had written on more than a dozen important American comics and looked back over my "findings" to see what patterns and configurations emerged. What I will be discussing, then, could be described as the theory of politics of the common man as found in comics. In some cases, such as *Pogo,* there is direct and outspoken (and even courageous) comment on specific political figures and events in American politics, but in most cases, we will be dealing with innate social and political philosophy.

It is these attitudes and values which give shape to American political life, which "condition" our political behavior, and if the comics do not as a rule focus upon specific issues in American politics, this does not mean that they lack a political dimension.

SPIRITUAL ORPHANS IN THE NEW WORLD PARADISE

By spiritual orphans I mean the notion, found in many American comics, that we have either been "abandoned" or that we lack, or have escaped from, history and the past; that we have cut ourselves off from our "motherland" and "fatherland." Loneliness is the price to be paid for freedom to create the future. Americans are cultural or spiritual orphans, free to create ourselves without the burden of a past or of institutions—but the cost is great.

Our very first comic strip, *The Yellow Kid,* reflects a strong sense of abandonment. The strip takes place in a mythical "Hogan's Alley," where a multitude of abandoned kids play. They are children but are not childish; many wear big derbies, some smoke cigars and cigarettes, others have beards, many are grotesque. They fill the frame (*The Yellow Kid* generally was not sequential but was instead a tableau) and reflect, in a subtle manner, the feeling Americans had at the time that they were to be overwhelmed by the spawn of Europe.

Outcault's style might be described as extremely "busy." Sometimes he had fifty or so characters in a tableau, as well as numerous animals, signs, posters, and speeches made by some characters. The *ambiance* was chaotic and bodies were inserted everywhere (sometimes hanging out on a line, like stockings which had just been washed). There was no place for "nature's nobleman," the American of the forest in this world; instead, it was peopled by tough little immigrant kids, Negroes with kinky hair, mangy animals, and despondent adults.

While most of the episodes in *The Yellow Kid* had a political dimension, in certain cases there was direct political commentary. The line between the political cartoon and the comic strip with political relevance becomes very blurred at times.

In one episode, done by Outcault's successor, George Luks, we see President-elect McKinley visiting Hogan's Alley. He stands in the foreground, majestic, holding two little babies in one hand and the Yellow Kid with his other hand. The walls are covered with bits of advice for "the major," written in dialect and, as was typical of the strip, misspelled. Another episode was devoted to the gold versus silver question which was important in the McKinley-Bryan election of 1896. In this cartoon, the Yellow Kid's robe contains the following statement, "fer O'Brien. At least I am inter politics."

Though *The Yellow Kid* is generally considered a humorous strip, beneath the absurdity and nihilism is a strong element of despair at the degradation of millions of Americans during the waning years of the nineteenth century. And yet there is also a certain kind of heroism in these kids, who are full of spirit and energy—and even social awareness—despite the awesome forces they must contend with. They have been abandoned, left to play in the alley, and must contend with a dehumanizing society, and yet they manage to maintain a sense of perspective and humor.

Many other characters in American comics are abandoned—or even orphans, both real and spiritual. Little Orphan Annie, Superman, Batman, Spider-Man... they are all orphans and their histories reflect with surprising accuracy important constellations of values in America.

LITTLE ORPHAN ANNIE

In Harold Gray's *Little Orphan Annie,* the distinction between the political cartoon and the comic strip disappears, for the strip is one long political diatribe in support of conservative values and politics. It is a legacy of the Coolidge era and was introduced (in 1924) when "The business of America is business" was the prevailing social philosophy. Gray sees the good society as a result of free competition by individuals in a laissez-faire ambiance, though Annie cannot explain how the selfishness of each (in a so-called free enterprise economy) leads to the welfare of all.

America is not what it should be—a paradise—and it is Annie's function to rail against the society in which she finds herself and to suggest that all is not lost, that there is a way for America to redeem herself. America has lost its way and the urban, complicated, cosmopolitan, bureaucratic, socialistic society in which she finds herself is a monstrosity that must be destroyed. America can be redeemed by liberating a dynamic force—the benevolent capitalist, the morally superior business-man. Freed from a destructive governmental bureaucracy, he can recreate the old, virtuous, simple America. Into the natural paradise of America the serpent of European ideas had glided, and when this snake is destroyed, we can return to the "good old days."

Given this ethos, it is only logical that the hero of this strip should be a titanic individual, one "Daddy Warbucks" (the name is most revealing) whose intrigues involve nothing less than the survival of the free world. Calling him "Daddy" humanizes him. Look, Gray is telling us, billionaires aren't that much different from anyone else, though there may also be an element of paternalism in the term. His real first name is Oliver.

And true to the dictates of the Gospel of Wealth, he is a servant of man and aware of the awesome responsibilities his great wealth imposes upon him. The strip has an aura of mystery and fantasy about it which suggests that Warbucks is the product of some kind of "higher law" which creates dynamic and heroic individuals like him. He always has special positions, secret missions, and we are to infer from his adventures that as a private individual he is able to avoid all the bureaucratic redtape which immobilizes our governmental officials. Daddy Warbucks engages in "direct action."

We are shown that history is a record of great men who transcend their societies and spend their time, in the case of the American experience, fighting foreign conspiracies. The strip reflects a diffuse paranoia to be found in many paramilitary groups; a sense that the enemy is everywhere, that the government is full of traitors, and that only a few people can be trusted.

In American society, which is egalitarian in terms of our value system, we have an economic but not a social or hereditary aristocracy (though we may be moving in this direction). Given this situation it can be seen what the basic function of Daddy Warbucks is—*mystification*. His role is to act as an apologist for capitalism, to suggest that those on the top are there on the basis of special capacities and virtues. And furthermore, that the only way to have a good society is to liberate these men so they can function efficiently. Yet the very ethos of the strip, which is full of desperate and pathetic "little people" contradicts this notion.

Indeed, *Little Orphan Annie* reflects the failure of what is probably the most important organizing myth in American culture, the myth of success and the self-made man, the so-called American Dream. Annie's tragedy is that she refuses to recognize the truth of this failure; her blank eyes cannot or will not acknowledge it.

Little Orphan Annie is really a prolonged morality play, a sustained jeremiad, exhorting Americans to return to "innocence" and implying that our salvation lies in a repudiation of Europe and history and institutions. Her confidence reflects another myth—that of the "chosen few" (in this case corporate capitalists) who will redeem American society. Annie's cause is hopeless, though, for she does not acknowledge the Great Crash, which destroyed America's faith in moral superiority of the businessman.

SUPERMAN AND THE PURITANS

Although there are other orphans and abandoned souls in the comics, I would like to conclude my discussion of this theme with a look at one of the greatest heroes of comicdom, *Superman*. Since Superman first appeared in 1938, he has changed in terms of his looks, his attitudes towards women and sex, the kinds of adventures he has had, and even his powers. But his significance as an American hero has not, and it is to this subject I would like to turn my attention.

The origin tale of *Superman,* the first two pages of the strip, is a remarkable reflection of the American ethos in an incredibly condensed but comprehensive form. *Superman is a pradigmatic hero whose experience recapitulates, so to speak, the American experience to an "extraordinary" degree.* He leaves a doomed planet, Krypton, just as the Puritans left a corrupt and destructive society, Europe. He becomes a real orphan. "Poor thing. . . It's been abandoned," says the woman who found him. The Americans become spiritual orphans who abandon their fatherland and the past. He had a "perilous" journey in an experimental spacecraft; and so did the Puritans and founding fathers, in their small ships. He comes to a new land where his powers are enormous. The same applies to the Puritans, who were free to set up a Holy Commonwealth, totalitarian theocracy, in which their powers were absolute.

Superman had a strong sense of mission. As the origin tale says: "Clark decided he must turn his titanic strength into channels that would benefit mankind. And so was created—Superman, champion of the oppressed, the physical marvel who had sworn to devote his existence to those in need."

The Puritans, likewise, had a strong sense of mission and believed that they would establish a perfect society which would lead to the eventual regeneration of mankind. Both had a single-mindedness that was quite remarkable, and both had a fear of the old world. Superman was weakened by exposure to fragments of his planet of origin, Krypton, and the Puritans feared (like countless generations of Americans after them) that exposure to old-world practices and ideas was morally corrupting and destructive.

Both Superman and the Puritans can be characterized as being

Superman and the American Experience

The American Experience	Superman
Leaves a corrupt land — Europe: Destructive Godless, not "pure."	Leaves a doomed planet, Krypton.
Becomes a spiritual orphan: Abandons fatherland, the past.	Becomes a real orphan: "Poor thing, It's been abandoned."
Perilous journey on small ships.	Perilous journey on experimental rocket.
Comes to new land — America.	Comes to new land — Earth (by chance USA).
Great Power Here: sets up city on a Hill; theocracy semi-totalitarian.	Great Power: Superhuman strength while on earth (can use strong-arm methods).
Sense of Mission: regenerate man.	Sense of Mission: use powers to help man.
Single-Mindedness: everything subjugated to mission.	Single-Mindedness: no sex, only work (until later on).
Fear of Corruption by Old World: European institutions, the past.	Weakened by exposure to Old Planet: Kryptonite (the past).
Psychological Complexity: Predestination and Willpower Effort-Optimism.	Psychological Complexity: Dissociated self; Clark Kent/Superman.
Super-Ego Society: Guilt, God punishes the evil.	Super-Ego Figure: no escape (even has X-ray vision).
Middle-Class Values: effort-optimism, strive and thrive.	Middle-Class Figure: Delayed Gratification Pattern, Forgo Fleeting Pleasures.
Inhuman Society crumbles: prosperity impossible strain.	Superhuman figure humanized: less square women.
Great Impact on American Culture: ideal of achievement, etc. values institutionalized.	Great Impact on Popular Culture: caped crusaders model for others.
Conservative Elements: self-reliant Individual saves self; willpower (Psychology) basic.	Conservative Elements: strong father saves, focus on superstructure not base?

psychologically complex (the Puritans with their belief in predestination and Superman with a dissociated personality). And both reflected the primacy of the super-ego. The Puritans had an obsession with evil, and Superman can be seen as a manifestation of this phenomenon. He is a supreme super-ego figure with super powers to punish wrongdoers. He was even given X-ray vision to seek out evil people no matter where they might be hiding. With Superman there is no escape.

The comparison can be extended further. Superman is an essentially middle-class figure who forgoes fleeting pleasures, as Nietzsche said supermen should, and attains "happiness and dominance through the exercise of creative power." This is quite close to the middle-class pattern of *deferred gratification,* and Superman is notorious (in his earliest supermanifestations) for avoiding sexual relations. Likewise the Puritans, with their effort-optimism, strive-and-thrive philosophy, championed middle-class values.

Superman, however, eventually became humanized and more complicated, and the Puritan experiment eventually crumbled, in part because it was based on an inhuman ideal and asked men to be what they were not—namely supermen. Also, increased prosperity seemed to weaken its grip on people. But Puritanism had an enormous impact upon the American psyche, and to a great degree, even to this day, its influence can be found in the basic American personality structure and in our values and beliefs. *Superman* also was formative: the first caped crusader was the model for later ones, though there have been great modifications in the kinds of heroes to be found in the comics.

Ultimately *Superman* is a conservative figure, for he focuses his attention upon problems of the superstructure, and not, to adopt Marxist terms, the base. He works like a demon, but he is always occupied with criminals and malfunctions at the most superficial level of society. He lacks political awareness and, at times, even verges on a kind of watered-down fascism, glorying in violence and direct solutions via a super bash in the teeth. He reflects the basically conservative views of the American public. We have, traditionally, posited the self-reliant individual as the means for achieving the good society; success is a function of willpower in a "just" society, in which people are not enslaved by traditions and institutions (such as royalty or the church).

The irony in America is that instead of a nation of individual supermen, we find a country full of seemingly powerless weaklings, full of fantasies of potency, while the state has become a superstate, with prodigious powers and, so it seems at times, a will of its own. The recent cataclysmic events in America surrounding the Watergate hearings have had a traumatic effect on the American political consciousness; the presidency has been demythologized and few Americans can maintain the fiction that the president is a combination of Superman and Jesus Christ Superstar, though once upon a time we tended to believe this.

ATTITUDES TOWARD AUTHORITY: NON-CONFORMISTS, GUNG-HO TYPES AND OTHERS

Generally speaking, as a consequence of our egalitarian ethos, most Americans can be characterized as "anti-authoritarian," and I have explored this theme in some detail in the first chapter of my *Li'l Abner.* In a comparative study of similar (in time of appearance and kind of hero) American and Italian comic strips, I discerned an important difference between American and Italian comics in terms of the way authority is treated. The Italian comics reflected a conservative approach towards experience and saw authority as valid and rebellion against it as futile. The American comics, on the other hand, had an "irreverential" approach towards authority, were much more "antisocial," and saw rebellious activity as having a strong possibility of being successful.

The dominant thrust in American comics is an anti-authoritarian or nonconformist one, though there are some strips, such as *Dick Tracy* and possibly *Batman,* which might be classified as authoritarian or, to use the vernacular, "gung ho." Probably it is best, and certainly it is safest, to see cultures as containing within them contradictions and engaging, in various ways, in dialogues about important issues. Certainly we find both positions or both points of view about authority in the comics.

Krazy Kat, George Herriman's brilliant strip (which is generally considered to be our greatest strip and the one which elevates the lowly comic strip into "art") is a case in point. The strip involves three characters: *Ignatz Mouse,* a malevolent, willful, egotistical, brick-throwing creature, who is always testing authority and generally paying the consequences for his antisocial behavior; *Offissa B. Pup,* a police figure, and the keeper of the jail where Ignatz spends much of his time; and *Krazy Kat,* a silly cat who loves Ignatz Mouse and interprets the bricks he uses to "crease" her noodle with as signs of love. Pup loves Krazy who loves Ignatz who loves to throw bricks, and for thirty years Ignatz threw bricks and Offissa Pup vainly tried to protect Krazy, whose passion grew greater with every knock on the head.

There are two important themes in this strip: the valuing of illusion (the brick as love) over reality and the attitude towards authority, which might best be characterized as one involving rebelliousness (on Ignatz's part) and an unwillingness to submit to authority. These two themes inform the strip, giving it an aura of poignancy.

Curiously enough, there is reason to believe that Herriman, the author of this strip, was a Negro who masqueraded as a white man. Thus the themes of illusion and rebelliousness stem from Herriman's personal situation and the difficulties he faced as a black man posing as a white. *Krazy Kat* can be characterized as an anti-authoritarian strip, for though Ignatz submits to superior power (in the form of Offissa Pup), he never admits the legitimacy of Pup's authority, and we always know that right after he gets out of jail he will heave another brick.

DICK TRACY'S PREOCCUPATION WITH EVIL

There is an officer, however, who represents a different attitude towards authority, an attitude which might be described as reverential or perhaps obsessional. *Dick Tracy* is about as far removed from the fantasy and mirthfulness of *Krazy Kat* as you can get. The *ambiance* of *Dick Tracy* is morbidity. A Calvinistic passion for scourging evil from the land pervades it. Chester Gould, who does the strip, has created a veritable bestiary of criminal monsters, grotesques, and freaks who succumb, inevitably, to Tracy.

He is activated by an overwhelming sense of purpose and seems to be a reflection of a super-ego of almost pathological proportions. The strip, drawn in strong blacks and whites, is permeated by a preoccupation with evil that is terrifying. He is a reflection of American evangelical Protestantism and stems from a long line of conscience-ridden Protestants who peopled the country, working strenuously to vanquish evil—in thought and deed. Tracy can be seen as a symbol of this tradition, which recoiled in horror at the evil in the world and threw up bloody avengers to root out the evil monsters who were trying to intrude into the American paradise.

Gould's use of grotesques is very significant. These figures are physically and morally ugly, and this facilitates a guilt-free aggression on the part of the readers. But are not grotesques creations of a grotesque society? Gould does not seem to consider this matter; he is too busy sending Tracy out in the relentless pursuit of criminals, a servant of a stern God striving to rid America of evil in the neverending quest for the sublimity of a community of saints. Alas, he never quite succeeds. Dick Tracy is probably an extreme instance, though the avenger is a common figure in American comics—but in comic books rather than comic strips, which are carried in newspapers and read by children as well as adults.

Batman is a good example of a comic-book hero motivated by vengeance. Like Superman, he too is an orphan and he too is engaged in a holy war against evil. As he says in his origin tale, "I swear by the spirits of my parents to avenge their deaths by spending the rest of my life warring on all criminals." I see Batman as a reflection of the pietist-perfectionist strain in American culture. This belief imposes upon each individual the responsibility to confront evil and try to root it out whenever possible. It has been described as: "the belief that every individual is himself responsible for deciding the rightness or wrongness of every issue (large or small) in terms of a higher moral law. . . and having made his decision, he must commit himself to act upon it at once, taking every opportunity and utilizing every possible method to implement his decision. . . ."

This is what creates the "crusader" and also leads to a widespread sense of guilt, since we cannot live up to such impossible ideals. In such a situation it is comforting to have a heroic fantasy figure who "redeems" us by his magnificent actions.

POGO AND McCARTHYISM

Unfortunately, this pietistic thrust frequently turns sour—in the case of McCarthyism, for example. Yet here too, in the face of this aberration, the comic had a role to play and the courageous satires of Walt Kelly in *Pogo* are thought to have had some role in helping to stem the hysteria that McCarthyism produced in America. Kelly attacked McCarthy in many episodes, portraying him as a lynx named Simple J. Malarkey, who becomes involved in all manner of nasty things. In one tale he leads an "anti-bird" campaign designed to protect the swamp, where Pogo and his friends live, from "unwelcome immigrants." This adventure had episodes involving book burning and attempts to "smear" innocent animals by tarring and feathering them—making them, in effect, birds.

But McCarthy wasn't the only politician Kelly satirized in his caricatures and fables. He drew Spiro Agnew as a creature that resembled a hyena, wore a military uniform like that of the Greek colonels, and talked an absurd gobbledygook.

In *Pogo* we find satirical and frequently nasty portrayals of other figures such as Richard Nixon, Lyndon Johnson, Bobby Kennedy, and Nikita Khrushchev. Kelly turns some of his characters into animals (George Wallace becomes a cock, Khrushchev a pig, Johnson a longhorn steer) and others into toys (Bobby Kennedy is shown as a wind-up toy man).

The Okefenokee Swamp is portrayed as a primitive paradise that is under attack from all kinds of evil characters—religious fakes, confidence men, political cranks, and fools, just to name a few. And it is Kelly's mission to present the American public with cautionary tales that have, frequently, very direct implications for American political life.

Kelly denies that he has a political stance or is trying to make a statement of any kind. All he wants to do, he claims, is "have fun and make money at the same time," but such denials are typical of humorists. By claiming they are not serious, they defend themselves from being attacked or sued by their "victims." In America it is also necessary to "take a joke," and dignifying an insult is a dangerous ploy.

I ought to mention a few other comics, if only in passing, before I conclude this discussion of authority and rebellion in the American comics. For a long time *Li'l Abner* was one of the most inventive and remarkable comic strips in America. It satirized and ridiculed, with brilliance and inventiveness, a large number of absurdities in American society—the predatory businessman, the stupid politician, gangsters, show business types, and so forth.

Al Capp, who wrote and drew the strip, was at the height of his powers one of America's most gifted satirists and social critics. Unfortunately, during the last ten years or so, his strip has lost its character. Capp has moved from a liberal to a conservative, and perhaps even reactionary, political stance.

The place Capp vacated as a liberal critic of American mores and politics has been taken by Gary Trudeau, whose *Doonesbury* is one of the most interesting new strips. The characters in *Doonesbury* are skeptical and iconoclastic, and Trudeau has been one of the most savage critics of Nixon. The strip is probably the closest thing in the American newspapers to the American underground comics, which attack American social, political, and sexual values and behavior with considerable severity and occasional wit. Interestingly enough, there was one series of episodes in *Doonesbury* in which one of the characters was banished to the garage by his father, who wanted to make money by renting out his son's room. Even in the 1970s we find American children being "abandoned" or rejected; it is not much of a move from the garage to the alley, which would complete the circle and bring us back to *The Yellow Kid.*

The popularity of *Doonesbury* leads me to believe that Americans are now reading newspaper comics selectively, for the same newspaper might carry both *Little Orphan Annie* and *Doonesbury,* which represent considerably different belief structures. What is happening in the newspapers is that the long serial adventure strips are losing their popularity and the "gag" strips are taking over. Thus *Orphan Annie* is an anachronism in philosophy and form.

There are, of course, many other strips which bear mentioning: *Mutt and Jeff, The Katzenjammer Kids, Popeye, The Wizard of Id,* and so forth. Fortunately, scholars in many different disciplines have "discovered" the comics in the last decade and serious attention is now being paid to them—not only in America but in many other countries.

CONCLUSIONS

While I was in the middle of writing this essay a cartoon by Feiffer appeared that is most relevant. One of his characters is delivering a monologue, which goes as follows: (Sunday *Observer,* May 19, 1974)

Someday. . .
There'll be a world without authority
Without bureaucracy
Without rules
Where there'll be freedom
and sharing
and love.
And still I won't fit in.

This cartoon deals with the two themes I've been discussing—the abandoned child/spiritual orphan and the rebel—and suggests their logical outcome, namely alienation.

For spiritual orphans have broken their ties with their fatherland, and those who will tolerate no authority can have few ties with their fellow man, and can never "fit in." Thus the anti-authoritarian spiritual orphan pays an enormous price for his so-called freedom; he is doomed to a kind of loneliness and solitude. Feiffer's character wants, it seems to "fit in" more than anything else. That is, he wants to be able to think of himself as a social person, as a member of something bigger than himself. Man is, after all, a social animal, and Americans, having rejected history and sacrificed the past to the future, often find themselves in a bind. When there is no authority, no bureaucracy and no rules, is there a society? Is there anything to "fit in" to? And is there, we might ask, freedom? Is a collection of alienated anarchists what the utopian dream of America is all about?

I think not, though if you push the themes of the spiritual orphan (voluntarily so) and anti-authoritarianism to their "logical conclusion" you do end up there. There is another side to this, which I have not dealt with, though my suggestion that cultures all engage in dialogues with themselves would indicate it. And as the great organizing myth of the self-made, self-created man disintegrates and reveals itself to be sterile, the communitarian myth, the myth of man as a social being, as a member of the family of man, grows stronger. The hunger of America for communes, for utopian societies, for voluntary associations is part of that side of the American personality, and it too is a part of the comics, though I have not time for it here.

The matter of the relation that should exist between the individual and society is a central question in politics. This question is dealt with explicitly and implicitly in the comics, in America and elsewhere. For the most part, Americans have thought they were being anti-authoritarian when they were only being antisocial. But things are changing! In America we have comics dealing with social problems, with ecology, with sexual politics, with almost any subject you might name.

As I write this a thousand new comic heroes are being born, to wage war upon a thousand fiends, and contribute to the education—political and otherwise—of all who follow their exploits. And who knows—somewhere, in some distant planet in some obscure universe of the American imagination, a new hero is speeding towards us, with new powers and a new social message. Will we listen?

Unflattering Definitions:

Significant Stereotypes in European
(French and Italian) Comics

I

In a remarkable but not very well known novel *Cards of Identity,* there is a scene in which a character of indeterminate sex is talking to a playwright. The playwright comments that he doesn't want to work on his play any longer and the following dialogue takes place:

"Then why not drop it?"

"How can I, dear? Don't be *too* obtuse. I must know who I am, mustn't I?"

"Surely your own play isn't going to tell you?"

"Of course not, dear; it's the critics who'll tell me. At the moment I don't exist; I don't even know what to *become.* But once my play's done, I'll know. One critic will say: 'Harold Snatogen reveals himself as an embodiment of the fashionable anti-Moon Goddess revival.' Another will say: 'In Snatogen we see what Hegel called. . .' and then he'll tell what Hegel called. After that it will be quite simple: I shall become the most flattering definition. . . ."

Snatogen then continues, a bit later:

"Oh, if only you were an expert on such matters. If only I could trust your judgment. But I need a more authoritative definition than yours. And it has to be *printed.* Speech is *useless.*"

This little scene deals with an important idea—that our identities are, in some ways, given to us by others (significant and otherwise), and frequently we are not so much able to create an identity as to select from the most flattering ones offered. But what about all the "unflattering" definitions of ourselves we are exposed to? How do they affect us, and what significance do they have?

If we concretize the term "definition" into something more tangible, such as stereotypes of Americans in the comics, we find ourselves with what I believe is a subject of considerable interest, and it is this matter that I propose to investigate. *I am, in particular, interested in stereotypes of Americans in European comics, though this is a complicated subject that necessarily will involve the matter of American self-stereotypes and the relationship that exists between stereotypes by Americans of Americans and stereotypes of Americans by non-Americans.*

My aim is not to determine what the basic stereotypes are (through some kind of massive content analysis of European comics), but rather to examine certain selected instances of stereotyping of Americans that I consider to be interesting and significant. I will deal with such matters as the source of stereotypes, the nature of stereotypes and the relationship between stereotypes and national character—as well as other related concerns.

This investigation will have not only a cross-national focus but will also have a cross-disciplinary perspective. The subject of stereotyping is a complex one. Comic strips and comic books are, themselves, also complex phenomena which can be analyzed from a number of different perspectives (sociological, aesthetic, psychoanalytic, historical, etc.) and which involve attention to graphic, narrative, and linguistic elements. (It is important to consider *aesthetic* aspects of comics and all forms of popular culture. Regarding popular culture only as a repository of values or examining it only in terms of incidences of violence, etc., often leads to oversimplifications and distortions. In many cases, "style" and the quality of "performance" are critical.)

In 1964 when I wrote my doctoral dissertation on *Li'l Abner,* I found the academic community hostile to the idea of paying serious attention to the comics. At that time the study of popular culture was not well developed and had little status; fortunately the situation has changed somewhat, and many universities and scholars have been forced to pay respect—still grudgingly done—to popular culture as a means of understanding man and society. I hope this study will be a contribution which will interest others and lead to further studies of the subject.

II

The term *stereotype* as we will use it is defined in *The Random House Dictionary of the English Language* (The Unabridged Edition) as follows:

> *Sociol.* a simplified and standardized conception or image invested

with special meaning and held in common by members of a group: *The Cowboy and Indian are American stereotypes.*

This definition is useful in that it implicitly connects stereotypes with media (which play an important part in spreading stereotypes). In printing we take one example and reproduce it many times; when we think in a stereotyped manner we take one person (or a few) and make generalizations about large numbers of people who are connected to that one person in some manner. We assume a kind of uniformity, which we get with print but do not get with people.

In Horton and Hunt's text, *Sociology,* we find another definition of stereotypes and some interesting points about this phenomenon:

> *Stereotypes* Outgroups are generally perceived in terms of stereotypes. *A stereotype is a group-shared image of another group or category of people.* Stereotypes can be positive (the kindly, dedicated family doctor), negative (the unprincipled, opportunistic politician), or mixed (the dedicated, fussy, sexless, old-maid school teacher). Stereotypes are applied indiscriminately to all members of the stereotyped group, without allowance for individual differences. Stereotypes are never entirely untrue, for they must bear some resemblance to the characteristics of the persons stereotyped or they would not be recognized. But stereotypes are always distorted, in that they exaggerate and universalize *some* of the characteristics of *some* of the members of the stereotyped group.

Although Horton and Hunt do not know how stereotypes begin, they offer some suggestions about how stereotypes maintain themselves:

> Once the stereotype has become a part of the culture, it is maintained by *selective perception* (noting only the confirming incidents or cases and failing to note or remember the exceptions), *selective interpretation* (interpreting observations in terms of the stereotype: e.g., Jews are "pushy" while gentiles are "ambitious"), *selective identification* ("they look like school teachers..."), and *selective exception* ("he really doesn't act at all Jewish"). All of these processes involve a reminder of the stereotype, so that even the exceptions and the incorrect indentifications serve to feed and sustain the stereotype.

This type of thinking—selective perception, selective interpretation, etc., correlates with low education, and quite likely there is a class element to stereotyping, especially when it involves racial, religious, and ethnic prejudice. Most scholars who have investigated stereotyping suggest that it is necessary, since people think in categorical terms. A stereotype is a generalization, a means of dealing with information that we are continually receiving and which we have to make sense of, one way or another. Of course, stereotypes are rather specific kinds of generalizations which refer to social groupings and which affect the behavior of individuals and groups, so they are not as "neutral" as the term *generalization* might imply they are.

Stereotypes are, in many ways, functional for individuals (though they may be dysfunctional for society at large) which might explain why stereotypes are so difficult to erase once they become popular. Some of the more important functions of sterotypes are as follows:

1. *Stereotypes rationalize group prejudice.* We have discussed this already and mentioned the different ways people distort reality to maintain their prejudices.

2. *Stereotypes create group cohesion.* They enable people sharing the same stereotypes to find commonalities which help give them an identity.

3. *Stereotypes separate people from one another.* People can disassociate themselves from others who are the "victims" of the stereotypes. People from groups with bad stereotypes may change the affiliations if the problems created by the stereotypes are severe enough.

4. *Stereotypes reinforce certain types of behavior.* In some cases, stereotyped groups adopt some of the stereotypes given them so that the stereotypes become "self-fulfilling prophecies." Thus, police who are called "pigs" may act more brutally (so as to fit the stereotype and continue it) than they would ordinarily act. To the extent that people tend to adopt the definitions of themselves given by others, stereotypes affect behavior.

5. *Stereotypes enable people to interpret the world and process information.* Stereotypes may be distortions, but they do enable people to make sense of the world and "understand" behavior. Thus, a person is "thrifty" *because* he's a Scot, or crude and vulgar *because* he's a middle-class American. And if he is a Scot, we can expect him to be thrifty, just as we can expect a person who is a middle-class American to be crude and vulgar—if, that is, we hold the dominant stereotypes of Scots and Americans.

6. *Stereotypes most commonly deal with social roles and related matters.* Social roles involve people's behavior in the world, and most of the stereotypes are concerned with behavior and expectations that people have of others relative to their position (status and group identity) in the world, in general, and in a given society, in particular.

Thus stereotypes enable people to understand behavior they see (or see selectively) and predict behavior (which, as we have pointed out, their stereotyping helps bring about).

The power of stereotypes is no doubt connected to their functionality for people who use them. Stereotypes tend to focus on the following topics: *personality, occupations, class levels, ethnic types, races, religions, nationalities, sexuality, cleanliness habits, foods, and intelligence.*

It is difficult to consider this list, partial as it is, without noticing that there is a striking similarity between the subjects that are frequently stereotyped by people and subjects dealt with in much of our folklore, jokelore, and popular culture, in general. Stereotypes are useful to writers and media people because they provide a kind of "instant" background and rationale of behavior for audiences. In this sense, stereotypes provide a theory of motivation which media people can use—they can rely upon them and, as they use them, can give them wider currency and reinforce them. The resemblance between the topics which are stereotyped and the concerns of humorists are particularly striking. If humor has a considerable amount of "masked aggression" in it, it is quite understandable that much humor (including folk humor as well as humor created by professionals) should involve stereotypes, since these stereotypes can be "tapped" for the aggression built up in them and discharged—creating laughter, a sense of relief, etc., via guilt-free aggression.

According to Alan Dundes, in his essay "A Study of Ethnic Slurs: The Jew and the Polack in the United States," there has been insufficient attention paid to folklore in investigating stereotypes. As he says,

> ... in examining the extensive national character and stereotype scholarship, one finds surprisingly little reference to the materials of folklore. Stereotypes are described almost solely on the basis of questionnaires or interviews in which an apriori set of adjectives, such as "honest" or "stingy," are assigned by informants to national or ethnic groups. One wonders, methodologically speaking, just how the researcher selects the initial list of adjectives and whether or not his personal bias in making up the list does not partially invalidate the results. [The fact that respondents are generally asked to select items from lists of paired opposites may lead to distorted and simplistic findings. Instruments such as surveys measure attitudes and opinions *about* popular culture rather than examining the works of popular culture themselves.] What psychologists and others fail to realize is that folklore represents an important and virtually untapped source of information for students of

national character, stereotypes, and prejudice. The folk have been making national character studies (that is, folk national character studies) for centuries.... The stereotypes are thus "already recorded" and would presumably be free from the inevitable investigator bias found in the unduly leading questionnaires.

Dundes not only points to the existence of a great deal of material which waits to be exploited, but also offers some suggestions as to the origin of stereotypes:

In the United States, as elsewhere, individuals acquire stereotypes from folklore. Most of our conceptions of the French or the Jew come not from extended personal acquaintance or contact with representatives of these groups but rather from the proverbs, songs, jokes, and other forms of folklore we have heard all our lives. The stereotypes may or may not be accurate character analysis; that is, they may or may not be in accord with actual, empirically verifiable personality traits. The point is, rather, that the folk stereotypes exist and more importantly that countless people make judgments on the basis of them. There is probably no other area of folklore where the element of belief is more critical and potentially dangerous, not only to self but to others.

What Dundes says about folklore, which he defines as "orally" transmitted material, can be said also about popular culture in general. Popular culture uses folklore (which is part of popular culture, in my opinion) and creates its own "poplore." It has the additional virtue of having a concrete existence (in print, film, videotape, etc.) which is accessible to the scholar. Thus, examining stereotypes in popular culture is important since popular culture plays such an enormous role in socializing people. This paper will deal with images of America in the comics both literally, in terms of the graphic images found in the comics, and figuratively, in terms of the meanings found in or behind the stereotypes. Now that we have an understanding of what stereotyping is and does, it is time to examine some stereotypes and analyze their significance.

III

The relation that exists between stereotypes in the comics and the "images" people have of nations represented by these stereotypes is a complicated one—and one on which there is considerable disagreement. In *Comics: Anatomy of a Mass Medium,* Reitberger and Fuchs raise the subject but do not deal with it in an extended manner. They say (p. 181):

Even in other types of comics [they had been discussing war comics] *the images of foreigners is almost always determined by national stereotypes.* Frenchmen have little Menjou moustaches, English-ment drop their "h's," the Germans belong to the blond Master race. Very often Germany is equated with Bavaria. All these cliche notions are also to be found in the translations. Producers have differing views about the image of America presented by American comics abroad. Bildschriftenverlag believes that comics can hardly influence the image of America held by young readers, but they could possibly deepen the picture of the pioneering period in Wild West comics which is conveyed to them in films and literature. Bulls Pressendienst believes "that comic strips could influence the picture of America which their readers visualize. In our opinion this picture is created in its essential aspects by other media like newspapers, films and television and mainly by news and social reporting" (my italics).

There is a certain amount of confusion in this passage, but there seems to be agreement on one point—that comics use stereotypes when dealing with people from various countries, and that they intensify, and perhaps reinforce, stereotypes picked up through other media, namely film, television, and the press. While I would agree that comics do intensify stereotypes, I'm not certain whether the other media have primary importance in generating stereotypes. If folklore is important in this matter, and if the earliest reading matter of children is important, then comics may play a far more important role than they are commonly given credit for.

In order to determine what are the most common stereotypes of Americans in European comics, I selected the following issues of the more representative comics: *Lucky Luke,* Vol. 1, No. 5, France; *Pilote,* No. 520 (Giant 10th Anniversary Issue), France; *Spirou,* No. 1645, France; *Il Giornalino,* No. 48, Dec. 7, 1975, Italy; *Pony Express,* No. 3, June 1976, Italy; *Ali Baba/Robinson,* Dec. 1967, Italy; *Tintin in America,* 1932, France. These issues were not selected according to any principle other than that of availability; I happened to have them in my library (in some cases, only the issue being studied). They are, I believe, a decent sampling of the more important comics, children's magazines of comics, etc., available in France and Italy—though the list could be considerably augmented with comics from these and other countries. (I will use French and Italian comics as typical of European comics in general in this paper.)

Since my concern here was with the *range* of stereotypes offered (which would lead to some kind of a "picture" or stereotype of Americans and American society), I did not count the number of times a stereotype was used. Rather, I tried to elicit the different stereotypes presented, both of Americans and non-Americans.

The most significant stereotypes are shown in the chart which follows. These stereotypes were elicited from examining the magazines listed in Chart 1.

To understand the importance of American stereotypes and themes in these comics magazines, which are produced locally (in France and Italy), it is useful to examine their contents. Limiting ourselves to the comics they carry, we find, for example, that the issue of *Il Giornalino* I selected has the following stories: (1) an Asterix adventure which involves red Indians; (2) an installment of The Last of the Mohicans; (3) several short episodes about a pink rabbit named Pinky; (4) "Tales of the Saloon" about red Indians and pirates, etc.; (5) an Italian translation of a Lucky Luke adventure, dealing with the American West. The issue of *Lucky Luke* magazine had the following comics adventures: (1) Joe Fast, FBI agent; (2) "The Legend of Alexis McCoy" (about the American Civil War); (3) a Lucky Luke western adventure about an itinerant goods and hardware salesman; (4) Aux Fous, which deals with French police; (5) a French adventure story called Tiriel; (6) a version of Goldilocks and the Bears turned into a Western adventure. The other magazines were more difficult to describe; none of them had the same amount of American material in them, though American topics (especially the West) and American themes were important.

This phenomenon of "Americanization" raises interesting questions. Why do the Italian and French magazines carry so much material, which they create themselves, dealing with American themes—and focusing upon the American West, in particular? This subject must have some kind of particular relevance to European children and young adults, who purchase these publications.

While I cannot answer this question, I can offer some suggestions. On the one hand, the American West may provide a fascinating and different fantasy world for young European children which appeals, in particular, to their needs for self-assertion and self-realization. I will develop this notion in more detail shortly (in my chart on the nature/culture bipolarity in the American imagination), but the thrust of my argument is that the American West provides a mythic world where individual initiative and willpower is efficacious, in contrast to the European mythic world where this is not perceived to be the case.

Second, and related to this notion, is the matter of familiarity with American popular culture and the whole question of our so-called "cultural imperialism." American films, television programs, fast foods, artifacts, and so on are popular in Europe (and many other cultures, too), and we may find that the comics magazines are cashing in

Chart I: Significant Stereotypes in European Comics Magazines

Lucky Luke	Pilote	Spirou

Indians
FBI agents
Confederate and
  Union soldiers
Cowboys (Lucky Luke)
 	
also:
French police
Roman soldiers
	Cowboys (Lucky Luke)
	
	also:
	Turbaned Baghdadians
	Pirates
	Negro cannibals
	Arabs
		Western police
		Comic Indians
		FBI inspectors
		
		also:
		Negroes in straw skirts
		Royal Canadian Mounted
		  Police

Il Giornalino	Pony Express	Ali Baba
Indians Cowboys Hunters (Forest men) Comic Cowboys (Lucky Luke) also: British Redcoats Romans (Asterix)	Cowboys Indians	Cowboys Detectives (Dick Tracy) American kids (Peanuts)

on this phenomenon. But in order to do this, of course, the programs must take care of certain needs and offer certain kinds of gratifications that other kinds of popular culture do not offer.

There may also be an element of wanting to identify with American society and culture in general, of wanting to be "modern" and progressive and all the other things that America stands for in the minds of many people (intellectuals often excepted). American society may be bourgeois, but that is the state that hundreds of millions of people in Europe and elsewhere yearn for. (Popular culture would be an instrument of mystification in the service of *embourgeoisement* for Marxist critics.) We might adapt the old song "How're You Going to Keep Them Down on the Farm after They've Seen Paris" by changing the last word to television (and films, etc.).

The listing in Table 1 deals with stereotypes based on easily identifiable phenomena, such as "occupation" or "race." (*The Random House Dictionary of The English Language,* The Unabridged Edition, defines *Indian,* or *American Indian* or *Red Indian* as "a member of the aboriginal race of America or of any of the aboriginal North and South American stocks, usually excluding the Eskimos.")

It is quite obvious (literally as well as figuratively) that a great deal of stereotyping is social and visual—that is, it focuses upon people who can be easily identifiable by virtue of their race, the clothes they wear, or something of that nature. There is a visual dimension to stereotyping in the comics; it is intimately connected to *physical appearance,* such as one's costume (cowboy) or race (redman). These matters, and perhaps the locale in which the various episodes take place, are the primary ways of establishing identity in the comics—as far as "nationality" is concerned, that is. (We are dealing here with *figure* and *ground* relationships. A cowboy figure located in a Western background provides maximum cues for readers. Westerns are *figure* stories, where lone individuals are all important, and American society is seen as a "figure" society in contrast to Europe and other "ground" societies, where traditions and institutions are dominant.)

What Chart 1 demonstrates is that European comics tend to focus upon a nineteenth-century America, an America of cowboys and Indians, of pioneers and trappers, with a few other stereotypes thrown in here and there. There are a number of reasons why this may have happened. First, and I have already alluded to this matter, cowboys and Indians are easily identifiable *figures.* Their clothes, the setting, and everything make instant identification possible. Second, this is a period when there was a great deal of "action," so that stories involving gunplay, scalping, and other forms of violence do not seem contrived. The myth of the West is that it was full of violence, so Western stories tend to have a great deal of violence in them. Third, there is the fascination of the American West for Europeans. It is known that there are many "Wild West" clubs in European countries, and the sale of Western-style clothes in France and other countries has reached astonishing levels. To many Europeans, curiously enough, being American (and identifying oneself, therefore, with progress and "the future") involves returning, in one's fantasies, to the nineteenth century and barren towns full of desperadoes. The popularity of baseball, a nineteenth-century pastoral sport, in some Asian countries (and the popularity of Western movies, etc.) leads me to wonder whether most foreign nations have a nineteenth-century view of American culture and society and are living—psychically—in our no longer existent frontier? Finally, of course, and connected with all of the above, there is the matter of the spread of American popular culture, and in particular, American films. They, no doubt, played a role in fixating (to such a remarkable degree) the European focus on America in terms of our Western heritage. The American Western film is, after all, an idiosyncratic genre, and to many people it is the Wild West that represents America and American character most truly.

To this I might add that there may also be certain unconscious reasons, involving such matters as jealousy and a desire to see Americans as wildmen and savages (or unmannered, crude, and unsophisticated types), which lead to a focus upon this period. It is wonderfully gratifying to people who might feel inferior, for one reason or another, to be able to visualize Americans as "primitives," lacking taste, style, culture, civilization, and so forth. And, I may add, who are we to blame the Europeans (or any others) if they choose to accept some of our least flattering self-portrayals or "definitions" of ourselves, as projected in our movies and other popular culture forms, as the "correct" ones?

The irony of the situation is that, curiously enough, the Europeans have "picked up" a picture which many Americans still have of themselves, although they are often not aware of this. What I am suggesting is that most Americans have a nineteenth-century mind and see themselves living in "Nature," much the way we believe the cowboys did. This, in spite of the fact that America is now an urbanized, bureaucratized, and industrialized society. To understand how this developed, we must return to America in the 1830s and examine the development of the American "world view" and, in particular, the "classical American identity." Most Americans, I would argue, have held on this *primal identity* even though it is a patently absurd one. This is so because this yields many gratifications and is intimately connected with our basic social and philosophical beliefs. (In this regard, Europeans may get double rewards: first, they can see us as unsophisticated primitives and feel superior; second, they can identify with us, vicariously, and derive a sense of the freedom, potency, and exuberance, which is associated with American culture and society.)

IV

In order to explain the "paradox" of the popularity of the Western and the dominance of Western-type heroic figures in the European comics I've examined, it is useful to consider some of the insights available to us thanks to the work of the structuralists. One of the basic concepts of structuralism is that meaning is derived from bipolar oppositions, such as poor-rich or savage-civilized. We are concerned here with the *paradigmatic* structure of a text, as contrasted with the *syntagmatic* structure, which focuses upon the arrangement of elements in a text. That is, we are concerned with what characters "mean" rather than what they "do."

Americans have tended to find their identity by contrasting themselves with Europeans, with their "fatherlands," and with everything connected with European historical society. When in other writings I suggested that Americans are antihistorical, I did not mean that America has no history. In fact, we have a significant proportion of all the historians in the world, and a large number of them spend their time writing about American history. What I mean is that we see ourselves as "beyond" history, as having "escaped from history," and being, instead, natural men living in a state of nature in a "new world paradise." That there is little basis in fact for these notions is beside the point. We see ourselves this way and have seen ourselves this way for a long time. Let me explain. I will be using the cowboy as a *signifier* and will attempt to explain what is *signified* by this image.

In the following list I would like to sketch out the basic polar oppositions existing in the American mind in the mid-nineteenth-century (and, to a large degree, to this day). The cowboy actually is a mediating figure who exists "in nature" between the red Indian, who lives in a state of savagery, and the cavalier (and other types), who lives in a debilitating state of civilization. Evil exists in both extremes: too much   nature (savagery) and not enough nature (society).

The primary opposition is between nature and culture; everything else stems from that opposition.

The concepts listed on the left, under "Nature," are those which Americans used to define themselves. They are based upon both a positive belief in America as "nature" and a repudiation of Europe as "history," which may account for the remarkable tenacity of these notions. We had to repudiate Europe to obtain an identity, but we were aided in the fact that we had so much "nature" to help us. The Western

Nature-Culture Polarity in the American Mind

NATURE	CULTURE/HISTORY
Cowboy*	Cavalier
America	Europe
The Frontier:	Institutions
Forest	Church
Free Land	Nobility
Natural Law, Rights	Custom
Freedom	Despotism
Innocence	Guilt
Timelessness	The Past
Hope	Memory
Paradise	Hell
Psychology	Sociology
Willpower	Class Conflict/Passivity
Rugged masculinity	Mannered effeminacy
Individualism	(The Crowd) Conformity
Agrarianism	Industrialism
Simplicity	Complexity
Wisdom	Training
Clean Living	Sensuality
Achievement	Ascription
Action	Theory
Equality	Hierarchy
Compromise	Ideology
Classless society	Class-bound society
The Sacred	The Profane
Nature Foods	Gourmet Cooking
Anarchy	Tyranny

*Note: The disappearance of the cowboy adventure from network television and his relative unimportance in American comics might mean that Europeans are suffering from a kind of *popular culture lag*. It also suggests that they are getting gratifications of some consequence from this figure—gratifications that we no longer get.

takes place in the waning years of the nineteenth century, when the frontier and nature were just about to give way to civilization. But civilization implies a kind of "Europeanization," so that the cowboy may represent the last authentic American hero. After him, the other heroes (such as detectives, for instance) have the stigma of history and society and are, then, "less American."

Thus the cowboy and his role-partners—the Indian, the trapper, the hunter, the frontier soldier, and all the others—are the best defined heroic figures for Americans, and likewise for Europeans, who may be interested, for novelty's sake (and some of the other reasons mentioned earlier), in finding an easily identifiable and authentically American heroic figure. (The matter is complicated by the fact that many non-American intellectuals [and some American ones, too, alas] contrast American society and culture, as represented by our *popular* culture, with their culture and society, as represented by their *elite* culture. This leads to stereotypes of Americans which are distorted, and non-Americans, which are also distorted.) The problem posed by the cowboy and all the other super-individualists is how to form a community with such people? Our dream is to create a "natural community," but this is a contradiction in terms. Thus, we define society as an "abstraction" which stands for an aggregate of individuals with no relationships among themselves, other than living in the same territory. The problems this matter of wanting to have our cake (nature) and eat it too (community) creates are enormous, and are at the root, I believe, of many of the social and political problems America faces.

Curiously enough, the conflict which I have described earlier between the "natural Americans" and "historical Europeans" continues in America, though in slightly different form. In *The Irony of Democracy: An Uncommon Introduction to American Politics* by Thomas R. Dye and L. Harmon Ziegler, we find the newest bipolar opposition:

> A major source of factionalism among America's elite today is the division between the new-rich Southern and Western *Cowboys* and the established, Eastern, liberal *Yankees.* This factional split transcends partisan squabbling among Democrats and Republicans, or traditional rifts between Congress and the President, or petty strife among organized interest groups. The conflict between Cowboys and Yankees derives from differences in their sources of wealth and the newness of the elite status of the Cowboys.

If we substitute European for Yankee, we have the nature/culture polarity I discussed earlier; we have "new wealth" versus "old wealth," as the authors explain matters:

> The Cowboys are self-made men who acquired wealth and power in an intense competitive struggle which continues to shape their outlook on life. Their upward mobility, their individualism, and their competitive spirit influence their view of society and the way they perceive their new elite responsibilities. In contrast, Yankees either inherit great wealth or attach themselves to the established institutions of great wealth, power and prestige. The Yankees are socialized, sometimes from earliest childhood, into the respon-

sibilities of wealth and power. They are secure in their upper-class membership, highly principled in their relationships with others, and public regarding in their exercise of elite responsibilities.

The battle has turned inward now and rages between the East Coast "aristocrats" (who more than likely are tainted by European ideas and culture) against the "Sun-Belt cowboys" (who are self-made men and arch-individualists). So in a sense, the *cowboy* still stands as a symbolically significant figure in American society, and the nineteenth-century American belief system still has great power in the mind of the twentieth-century cowboy, just as it did in the mind of his nineteenth-century counterpart.[1]

To this point, I have concerned myself with what the basic stereotypes of Americans are, and in particular, I've focused upon one of the dominant figures found in European comics (at least the ones I've examined), the cowboy. It is useful to examine a typical adventure to see how this figure is portrayed in the comics. Is a cowboy in a French or an Italian comic adventure really an American figure (in terms of his values, beliefs, attitudes, etc.) or is he a Frenchman or Italian who happens to be wearing cowboy clothes?

The Lucky Luke adventure entitled "Le Colporteur" is a typical story. It begins with a robbery, in which a hardware and goods man named W. Flatshoe is being held up by two bandits. Before they can get any money from him, two shots ring out and their guns are shot from their hands. The robbers gallop away and we find Lucky Luke, mounted on his white horse, holding a smoking gun. Flatshoe asks Luke if he wants a reward and offers some gifts. Luke refuses any reward but mentions he is tired. Flatshoe invites Lucky Luke to lunch and serves him a gourmet dinner on a fine tablecloth with wine glasses, champagne, and so on. The next morning, when they set off for town, they are attacked by Indians. Lucky Luke runs out of ammunition but Flatshoe has boxes of bullets as well as rockets, which Luke uses to summon the infantry. Luke is able to prevent a confrontation between the army and the Indians; he discovers that the Indians were on the warpath because their bisons were massacred by some white men. Flatshoe, meanwhile, makes a deal to purchase Indian blankets, and afterwards everyone smokes a peace pipe (with tobacco supplied by Flatshoe). Lucky Luke rides off into the sunset singing "I'm a poor lonesome cowboy and a long, long way from home...."

The story is basically comic, though my description doesn't bring this element out as well as I might have done. It was written by Rene Goscinny and drawn by someone named Morris (only that name is given), and Morris's style is basically a humorous childish one.

Characters have big noses, skinny legs and large feet. It is all rather funny, especially the fact that the "colporteur" has everything on hand that is needed for anything. As such, Flatshoe represents a picture of Americans as extremely practical, adaptive, innovative, and ingenious. At the end of the story, as a matter of fact, there is an explanation that men like Flatshoe helped conquer the West, that Flatshoe and his sons have 120 stores, etc. Flatshoe is shown to be a sharp businessman, but he is not unscrupulous by any means and performs a service to society. On the other hand, everything he had has a price attached and he can be interpreted as a symbol of American "materialism" and ambition, though this "materialism" is beneficent.

This story certainly casts the cowboy as a positive figure and shows America in a good light, even though there was the holdup and the difficulty with the Indians. The West is posited, we must recall, as a wild place, and it is not unusual to find robbers and such there.

The landscape scenes are particularly significant here; a high percentage of the frames show *horizon lines,* which is important in terms of giving a sense of spatiality and openness. This, in turn, can be connected to ideas about opportunity and self-realization which Americans (and perhaps Europeans, also) see as possible in nature and in natural settings, where there aren't institutions to hold people down. This can be seen in the story where we find that Flatshoe becomes a big success and ends up with a number of stores in American, and ultimately in Europe too.

There are some aspects of the story which are a bit strange and which indicate that this is a foreign version of an American genre. For example, the scene where the "colporteur" serves an elegant gourmet meal with champagne is a bit farfetched and out of context. There is also the matter of the use of the French verb form, *vous,* which is something of a problem here, since it is used as an indicator of deference and contrasts with the American egalitarian "you." Americans, who are easy going and informal, as a rule, would not use the *vous,* yet the use *tu* would seem quite inappropriate to French children. Also, Lucky Luke is generally shown with a cigarette hanging out of his mouth, and this would not be condoned in a typical American comic strip in that it would provide unsuitable role modeling for readers of the comics.

Since the plot is a basic one of the Western—it might even be called a formula—the narrative structure is typically American, but the characters seem to relate to one another more in French terms than American. In any case, both Luke and Flatshoe are positively viewed, though one could read an implied criticism of American culture in the stories as one of emptiness and violence. As a stereotyped American, Lucky Luke is heroic and admirable, and offers a positive image of American culture and society.

V

I will conclude this investigation of stereotypes of America (and Americans) in European comics with a case study of an important French-language comic-strip hero, Tintin. Tintin is done by a Belgian artist, Hergé (whose real name is George Remi) and is now a comic hero of universal significance, probably one of the most popular and important children's comics published in Europe. His only rival would be Asterix. Both are published in book format, with a typical Tintin adventure—such as the one I will discuss, *Tintin En Amérique*—being sixty-two pages long.

According to Pierre Couperie and Maurice C. Horn's *A History of the Comic Strip,* Hergé has published twenty-one books dealing with Tintin's adventures in countries from Russia to Tibet to America, plus many children's books and other works. There is a journal called *Tintin: The Journal of the Young from 7 to 77 Years of Age,* which appears regularly and which has a variety of heroes in it, including Tintin. Finally, European scholars, who take an avid interest in the comics as repositories of social and political values, have devoted considerable attention to Hergé's works, with interesting results. A book edited by Charles-Olivier Carbonell, *The Social and Political Message of the Comics,* has articles on Tintin exploring such questions as: is he a fascist and a racist, has Tintin become a myth, and so on. The analysis of Tintin that I will make here will not concern itself with such questions—which are legitimate—but with images of America and Americans in *Tintin En Amerique,* which was published in 1932.

The cover of *Tintin in America* (I will use English translations henceforth) shows Tintin tied to a stake in an Indian village, while a ferocious looking Indian chief, tomahawk in hand, points to him. The title page shows Tintin in a cowboy's outfit riding a horse, while Milou, his faithful and remarkable white dog, holds on for dear life. So there is a basic image of America that is presented by the cover and title page which is the America of the West, which I've discussed earlier.

There are four basic stereotyped figures in the book—policemen, cowboys, Indians, and gangsters. A content analysis of the sixty-two pages of the book shows that these figures dominate *Tintin in America,* and the extent to which they do so is shown in Chart II.

The figure for gangsters is high because Tintin's main antagonist, a gangster, appears in adventures taking place in the Wild West and other places.

The generalization that emerges from this portrayal of America is one of the radical opposites. It is a world split between the gigantic metropolis of Chicago, where the police salute the gangsters (who dominate the city), and the Wild West, where Indians and desperadoes of varying sorts live. But it is also a country that is full of antisocial beings—some who are "civilized" and others who are savage or wild and can be misled.

Chart II: Stereotyped Figures in "Tintin In America"

Figure	Gangster	Cowboy	Indian	Policeman
Number of Pages in Which Appear	37	11	7	16
Percentage (approx.)	59%	17%	11%	25%

As early as 1932, as *Tintin in America* graphically demonstrates, the image of America (in comics) that existed in the French-speaking portions of Europe (and probably other areas also) was not too far removed from what it seems to be today. That is, America is still seen as a kind of mythical land populated by stereotyped figures—gangsters, cowboys, and Indians. In short, the stereotypes which I found in the contemporary French and Italian comics are basically the same ones found in *Tintin in America,* published some forty years earlier. (If there is any new heroic American type, it may be the astronaut—our newest symbolic figure, who also has the virtues of being easily identifiable and widely publicized, thought the Russians also have astronauts, so the figure is not exclusively our own.)

Some psychologists have suggested that there is a law of "primacy" which holds that first impressions tend to color all subsequent ones. This would suggest that the earliest stereotypes of American society—the cowboys, Indians, and gangsters—represent America, or perhaps the "mythic America" of the Europeans. It is a world that is distinctive and different, populated (especially in the case of cowboys and Indians) with easily identifiable and romantic figures whose grasp on everyone's imagination remains powerful to this day. Children would be exposed to these figures at an early age, and their views of American society would be influenced by such characters.

Tintin in America is a clever combination of a detective story and a cowboys and Indians adventure. I have explained the significance of the disappearance of the Westerns in American television programs as follows (in my *TV-Guided American*):

> The Western appeals to us because it is prepolitical and prebureaucratic; it is an empty vessel of *potentiality* into which we can pour an infinite number of different plots, mythic heroes, character types, settings, stereotypes, themes and so forth. We can still dream about creativity in nature and the possibility of establishing our own "natural" institutions. That dream has faded and we now see ourselves as prisoners, hostages of an overwhelming and de-individuating urban environment in which the goal is not so much self-creation but survival.

This may also be the basis of the tenacity with which the Europeans have held on to the stereotypes of America as a land of gangsters, cowboys, and Indians. It may be more correct for young children to play cops and robbers rather than cowboys and Indians, but as any child can tell you, it isn't more fun.

VI

The images which French and Italian children (and European children in general) have of America are quite unrealistic, and are often even a century out of date. These images remain powerful because of the reasons I mentioned earlier and also because of the capacity of popular culture to affect people's views. People who watch a great deal of television tend to assume the world is much more violent then it really is. This is because they are exposed to so much violence on television that they assume real life is equally violent. In the same light, popular culture conveys certain images of America and tends to focus upon certain types of heroes, neglecting a great deal that would give people a more balanced view of American society.

One of the complications here is that many elitists (Americans and non-Americans alike) tend to judge American society on the basis of its popular culture and other societies on the basis of their elite or folk culture. This is not correct, but it is easy to do since American popular culture is so all-pervasive. There seem to be few countries that have not been reached by McDonald's hamburgers, Kentucky Fried Chicken, Coca-Cola, pizza stands, American films and television shows, *Peanuts,* and so on. This is what is most available to people and what tends to shape their perceptions of America. Other people judge us by our soldiers—sometimes from World War II—and tourists, neither of whom are our best or most typical or best representatives.

All of this leads to distortions and absurdities; when you add the problems of communication created by different languages, customs, traditions, and political orientations, it is no wonder that the stereotypes of Americans tend to be negative, and from my point of view, often quite mistaken. (Many Americans, in the same light, have distorted views of their own country and other countries as a result of stereotypes we have about Englishmen, Frenchmen, Italians, and so on.)

This leads me to conclude that study of popular culture is a complicated matter and our entertainments and other aspects of popular culture which seem so common and ordinary and trivial are, in fact, extremely difficult to deal with. Thus the images we find in popular culture are filtered through the consciousness of artists and writers, audiences, media people, etc., and are affected by media limitations and the sociopolitical order of the countries in which popular images are created and disseminated. The cowboy, for example, is a signifier which signifies different things, almost certainly, to Americans and European—though there are, no doubt, certain ideas and gratifications which both Americans and Europeans derive in common from this figure.

Images and stereotypes of Americans found in the comics (or any other form of popular culture) do not tell us everything about how we are perceived abroad, but they tell us a great deal. Bishop Berkeley wrote that "to be is to be perceived." We can switch that around somewhat and say that, for most people, Americans are assumed to be as they are perceived, and, for the ordinary person, it is popular culture more than anything else which shapes these perceptions.

NOTE

1. If we accept the notion that images are important, we ought to consider where we find these images, how they are created and transmitted, how they are received and perceived, etc. We may find a number of different aspects to consider and should not assume that images simply exist! Thus we have *artists* (who create images), *works of popular culture* (which give the images shape), *audiences* (who perceive images selectively and often interpret them selectively), and the *society at large* (which generates images). There is also, in many cases, the *media* (which transmits the various forms of popular culture). The relationship that exists among all these phenomena is complex; we must locate where the images and stereotypes we are talking about when we talk about images are to be found. They are not *sui generis* and don't always have the same meaning and significance.

SELECTED BIBLIOGRAPHY

Berger, Arthur Asa. *Li'l Abner: A Study in American Satire*. Twayne Publishers, New York. 1970.

_____. *The Comic-Stripped American*. Walker & Co. New York. 1974.

_____. *The TV-Guided American.* Walker & Co. New York. 1976.

_____. *"The Politics of Comics,"* in *Crimmer's: The Journal of the Narrative Arts.* Spring, 1976.

Carbonell, Charles-Olivier. *Le Message Politique et Social de la Bande Dessinée.* Private. Toulouse. 1975.

Couperie, Pierre, and Maurice C. Horn. *A History of the Comic Strip.* Crown Publishers. New York. 1968.

Hergé. *Tintin En Amerique.* Casterman. Paris. 1931.

Reitberger, Reinhold, and Wolfgang Fuchs. *Comics: Anatomy of a Mass Medium.* Little, Brown and Co. Boston. 1971.

Dagwood in the American Psyche

Blondie was one of the most popular, if not the most popular, American comic strip until the meteoric rise of *Peanuts* in recent years. Dagwood Bumstead, as many commentators have pointed out, is an infantile, weak, greedy, and incompetent figure. As Marshall McLuhan put it in *The Mechanical Bride:*

> Dagwood is a supernumerary tooth with weak hams and a cuckold hair-do... is seedy, saggy, bewildered and weakly dependent.... He is an apologetic intruder into a hygienic, and save for himself, a well-ordered dormitory. His attempts to eke out some sort of existence in the bathroom or the sofa (face to the wall) are always promptly challenged. He is a joke which his children thoroughly understand. He has failed but Alexander will succeed.

McLuhan sees Dagwood as assuming a "little-boy role" under the pressure of Blondie's "mothering wedlock" and goes on to relate the strip to Margaret Mead's notions about the third generation in America being the one that will succeed.

Others have noticed the same thing in *Blondie*. Geoffrey Gorer, in *The American People,* said, "Although naturally exaggerated, Dagwood does represent a very widely spread attitude toward the American man as husband and father. Dagwood is kind, dutiful, diligent, well-meaning within his limits; but he has so completely given up any claim to authority that the family would constantly risk disintegration and disaster, if it were not for Blondie." This attitude toward the American male has, in recent years, crystallized in the disappearance of fathers from situation comedies on television, or, in some cases, of mothers. Having a missing father makes romance more possible while allowing the domestic comedy to continue.

Dagwood Bumstead is an important archetype in the American psyche: the irrelevant male. He is still in the strip, but he is only there as an object of ridicule and a symbol of inadequacy and stupidity. His job was breeding, and now that that is done with, and Alexander and Cookie produced, he remains on as a fool who is the butt of many jokes.

His name is absurd, the name of an irrelevant person, a clown. Bumstead is silly; perhaps it is close to bump and to lump, which suggests, perhaps, lumpenproletariat. Bum also means "tramp" and rear end, neither of which are flattering. (Strange to think that the offspring of this "nothing" would be named Alexander, the name of a conquerer of the world.) His face, with those two dots for eyes and the hair standing out in two tufts, as if they were horns and he were cuckolded, is ludicrous, and even more so since Blondie is relatively realistically drawn, often with a good bit of leg showing. Actually Dagwood's face has changed from the first strips, when he was a rich young man and was portrayed more realistically. Now, with the cuckold hairdo, he represents an ancient tradition in comedy: the man whose wife has been unfaithful to him but is unaware of it. This humor is based on exposure and ignorance—we know something Dagwood doesn't. And Dagwood's general inadequacy at the job and around the house fits in well with the notion that he is probably inadequate in the bedroom.

Since he has no sex life, he gains his satisfaction through gluttony. The kind of sandwich he made famous, the Dagwood sandwich, is a hodgepodge of leftovers in the refrigerator all wedged in between two slices of bread. Food seems to be his only real source of gratification, which suggests that he is a case of arrested development, never having left the oral stage for the genital. In that sense, he is a child himself, and assuming the little-boy role should not be very difficult for him.

There are, of course, certain limitations necessitated by the domestic comedy. The sources of humor must be relatively obvious, tied to family doings, and over *seemingly* harmless and trivial events. But beneath the lightheaded and rather simple-minded humor of the strip, which uses exaggeration and error as two basic modes of operation, there is the theme of the irrelevant male who is an object of humiliation. Dagwood has been disinherited, is browbeaten by a domineering and assertive wife, is abused by his boss, and is generally a failure in everything he tries, although his intentions are often generous and he means well.

The fact that *Blondie* got started in the height of the depression may have some significance. It was a period when our faith in the businessman was just beginning to founder, when the country was in the midst of a terrible depression, and when the average workingman, still imbued with the self-made man myths, saw *himself* as ultimately responsible for his dire predicament. It has been suggested, in fact, that the comics filled the gap in providing models for instruction and entertainment left by the decline of the Horatio Alger story.

Dagwood's decline, then, mirrors a sense of inadequacy and irrelevance and, in particular, powerlessness that was quite widespread in American society. After his fall from power as the son of a rich man making merger plans all the time, to a disinherited, castrated family man, he takes on the semblance of a clown. His life is one of continual ignominious defeat, masked by a thin veneer of geniality and slapstick buffoonery. But there he is: a man who hates his job, is abused by his wife, and is the butt of a thousand jokes. There is almost a heroic dimension to Dagwood Bumstead—he refuses to be destroyed—but he is not truly heroic because he lacks self-awareness and self-understanding. Thus he is pathetic and not tragic.

The change in his looks marks graphically his decline into irrelevancy, and with him, perhaps, the decline of the American male's sense of adequacy and potentiality.

An early strip is most instructive. Dagwood introduces his fiancée, Blondie, to his father. He brings her to his father's office. The father says, "But son I'm awfully busy . . . I'm working out plans for this new merger." Dagwood says, "But pop . . . I want you to meet Blondie . . . we're engaged you know . . . This is Blondie, Dad—she's awfully bashful and shy . . . you'll love her." Blondie says, "Oh tee hee . . . I always feel so boo-boop-a-doop when I meet my boyfriends' papas. . . . *But I usually like them better than the sons . . .* [my emphasis]. Can't I call you 'pop' Mr. Bumstead? Tee hee." Dagwood says that they have to leave so as to give his father time to work out his plans for his "new merger." Blondie responds, "Oh pop . . . if you aren't the terror! What are you going to do with your old wife?" She has misinterpreted what Dagwood meant by "merger," which is the source of the humor in this day's strip. There is a certain element of aggression in the phrase "old wife" and a hint of what is to come in marriage with her revelation that she likes her boyfriends' fathers better than their sons.

In this early strip, Dagwood is a young playboy-type who seems to lack any notion of what is in store for him when he is married. A look at Dagwood in later episodes shows an entirely different scene—the one we are familar with—which is based on the notion that marriage is debilitating and destructive of virility and masculinity. This has now become a veritable cliché in the comics and in popular culture in general. (Charles Winick has pointed out that romantic love in advertisements seldom involves marriage partners; it takes place during courtship and amongst single people.)

Dagwood's attempts to retreat are also futile. He takes to the sofa with his face hidden from the reader in an attempt to find a bit of peace and quiet, some solitude. But these attempts are not successful. He cannot evade Blondie's dominance. The relationship between Dagwood and Blondie is a parody of that existing in many families, in which there is a domineering figure who tends to do the decision making (and "holds the marriage together") and a passive figure who is acted upon, subservient, and submissive. Except that it does not seem possible for this kind of a relationship to exist without various attempts, on the part of the passive figure, to assert himself, gain some kind of psychic equilibrium, and perhaps, in some subversive way, control things.

Dagwood's inadequacy is a form of control, for Blondie must take care of things, run the house, solve the problems, whatever has to be done. What we find in Dagwood is a form of "aggressive passivity" that he uses as a tool of domination. This aggressive passivity takes a number of forms, such as Dagwood's not doing certain things that are expected of him, his being "overwhelmed" and rendered incapable of doing things, and his refusal to acknowledge what is expected of him and, thus, remaining "free" not to act. It is a form of control by weakness and purposive inadequacy.

If Dagwood Bumstead is an irrelevant male, a bumbling fool who cannot be counted upon to do anything adequately, it is, in part, because he "chooses" to be so at great cost to his sense of self and self-esteem. In a sense he has made Blondie into what she is. In many families the same tragic pattern of active and passive aggression is repeated, in the same way as in the strip, with disastrous results all around. In this respect, Blondie is as much sinned against as sinner, and her "mothering wedlock" is not entirely a matter of her own choosing, as is the case in many families.

The widespread popularity of the strip signifies, I believe, some kind of a subliminal awareness on the part of the readers of *Blondie's* actual relevance. *Blondie* is the most popular comic strip of domestic relations in America, and one reason for this is that the readers can see beneath the humor and recognize their own patterns of behavior being acted out, even if this is done in a highly exaggerated and zany manner. The humor, after all, is often quite bland and not particularly effective. Thus it is unlikely that the humor of each strip is what interests readers. The probability is, rather, that the representation of rather pathetic domestic relations cloaked in exaggeration and absurdity really intrigues us. In *Comic Art in America,* Stephan Becker says that Dagwood "wins" about 15 percent of the time. This is not a very good batting average, but is necessary to maintain a mild element of suspense. The basic question we ask ourselves when we read *Blondie* is—*how* will Dagwood be ridiculed? We know what to expect; we don't know how it will be done.

It may be that one of Dagwood's functions for us, as readers, involves his inadequacy, which makes us so much superior. He reassures us, in a sense, that we are not alone and not as bad as some. And in the strip, we are allowed to watch with fascination a low-keyed (in terms of awareness on the part of the participants) enactment of our own domestic tribulations and tragedies. Dagwood is irrelevant because he has no interiority, no soul, and no adequately developed male identity. He is shown in one episode as nothing but a source of money for Blondie—who goes on a spending jag. Perhaps one of the reasons for Dagwood's plight, aside from the fact that contemporary American society offers no adequately delineated male identity, is that he is so good-natured and willing, at all times, to see the humor in situations. He even makes light of his being mined by Blondie—because he has been taught, like all of us, to be "a good Joe."

This pose of good-naturedness reflects an unwillingness to face problems, to become angry or upset. It is one of the basic role-myths in American culture to be cheerful and to avoid showing how you really feel. What happens, ultimately, is that the pose takes over and we lose the capacity to feel or, at least, to admit our feelings to ourselves. This, in turn, leads to the repression of feelings which, in real people, often manifest themselves in destructive ways.

Many American males are currently struggling with the problem of attaining a useable male identity. As the Marlboro advertisements show, we still tend to see the male as a rough and tough figure from the frontier—a heritage of the past—which does not help much since we are now an urbanized and bureaucratic society, and one in which there is a great deal of desexualization going on. (This is the argument of Charles Winick in *The New People.*) The situation becomes exacerbated when you have the men (and the women) locked in the kind of familial relationship portrayed in *Blondie*.

Dagwood Bumstead lacks ego strength. He does not recognize the damage that is being done to him (or has been done to him) due to his notion of how he should conduct himself and how he should relate to his wife and children. Exploited (and exploiting, in his own subtle way), abused, depersonalized, and all but destroyed (in great part because of a fear of rejection), Dagwood is in the tragic situation of being an irrelevant male and feeling it, but not knowing it. To the extent that he is an archetype for American men, who find that many of the situations in the strip somehow "strike a chord," it is a tragedy of the most profound dimensions.

Part 3

Television

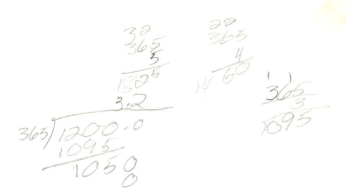

Television as an Instrument of Terror:

A Theoretical Prospectus

INTRODUCTION

Generally when we think of television, we classify it as an entertainment, and once in this logical category, we dismiss it as "harmless." We all say that television is frequently dull, banal, boring, that it feeds upon escapist needs we have (how did we get them?), and enables people to live "vicariously," if that is not a contradiction in terms? But television's very softness, its cool glare (which has become so much a part of our lives), its all-pervasiveness tend to make us lose sight of its power. The measure of television's power is that hardly anyone is aware of it—though people may watch it 3 or 4 or 5 or more hours per day. (The average person in America watches TV 1,200 hours *per year* and spends 5 hours *per year* reading books, according to Jerzy Kosinski.)

Television is no longer a miracle. It has permeated our lives and now is as necessary a part of our media regimen as the newspapers and radio. Young people born before television cannot imagine what life was like before it existed. Was there life before television? Is there life after television?

There is, obviously, but it has been changed radically. Before television there was political terror; afterwards the stage was set for psychic terror as well as other kinds. And, as I shall point out, television is also a subversive agency which can, almost in spite of itself, subvert the state.

TERROR

Terror is defined in *The Random House Dictionary of the English Language* (The Unabridged Edition) as "intense, sharp, overmastering fear," which lists as synonyms: horror, panic, and fright. These definitions and understandings do not do justice to the term, however, for they always suggest a specific object which creates the fear leading to the terror, or vice versa. Unsatisfied with this definition, I consulted several psychiatric dictionaries, neither of which had terror listed. (One had "night terror" or *Pavor nocturnus,* which it described as "a disorder allied to nightmare, occurring in children. . . . There is *complete amnesia* for the attack as well as for the dream content." This is not adequate but does give us something to think about.)

It is more useful to think about terror in terms of the goals of terrorists: disorientation, paralysis, confusion, debilitation, as well as fear. (Traditionally *terror* is understood to be used by the powerful, by the state, and *terrorism* is seen as an instrument of the powerless. The terrorists I am talking about here are the people who control society [and the media] as well as those who attack it.) Terror is an instrument used to mobilize people, collectively, while its long term result (as I shall use the term) is to pacify them, individually. There is always a dialectic in terror. We find it in the divergence between the goals of terrorists (peace) and their means (violence); between the compulsion found in television and its seeming innocuousness and triviality.

THE RECONSTRUCTION OF REALITY
WHILE VIEWING TELEVISION

Viewing television is not the same as watching a film. A film is a collection of discrete images, each one within a frame, which pass before our eyes in rapid succession. The frames are projected at approximately one-fiftieth to one-seventy-fifth of a second, so that when we watch a film we are seeing a succession of images alternating with blankness; our eyes are tricked by the succession of images and a collection of still images is seen as having motion. The screen is empty approximately half the time but it is not perceived as such, just as the static images are not perceived as such.

Television viewing is much different. As Tony Schwartz describes the process in *The Responsive Chord:*

> A television set creates a visual image by projecting dots of light, one at a time, onto the front screen. The succession of dots move across the screen and down alternative "lines." In all, there are 525 such lines on American television sets. During each one-fifteenth of a second, the scanning process will have completed two sweeps, once on each alternate set of lines.

> In watching television, our eyes function like our ears. They never see a picture, just as our ears never hear a word. The eye receives a

few dots of light during each successive millisecond, and sends these impulses to the brain. The brain records this impulse, recalls previous impulses, and expects future ones. In this way we "see" an image on television. The process differs from film in that it requires much faster processing of information and more visual recall (pp. 14-15).

He adds that while the brain "has to process twenty-four distinct inputs per second" with film, with television it "has to process thousands of distinct inputs per second" and it has to "fill in (or recall) 99.999 percent of the image at any given moment, since the full image is never present on the screen."

Television presents us with an incomplete world and forces us to reconstruct it continually. In ordinary life, the images that we see are full and stationary; they are there for us to contemplate, and they supply a coherent set of stimuli for us. Film moves us away from this—we see a succession of "still lifes," so to speak, which take on motion as a result of optical illusions. But television is the furthest removed from everyday life; here we find ourselves bombarded with dots in mosaic form which we must construct, at every moment, to create images that we can recognize.

When Marshall McLuhan talks about television being a "cool" medium, he is referring to this characteristic of television viewing. The television image is low in data and forces the viewer to become involved and make sense out of the data available to him. As he writes in *Understanding Man,* "TV is a cool, participant medium," and it is—in terms of our need to fill in gaps among dots. As far as program content is concerned, that is another matter.

I like to make a distinction between a medium, which is a channel, and popular art forms, which are carried on the channel. Television is a medium which carries a wide variety of popular art forms, such as the detective story, commercials, news programs, soap operas, situation comedies, and so on. (I have dealt with the social and cultural significance of many of these genres in my *The TV-Guided American,* Walker, 1976.) In the sections of this paper that follow, I will discuss television as an instrument of terror in terms of both television's "sensory" or formalistic qualities as well as its programmatic ones, for both the medium and its programs are instrumental in creating what I call terror.

DISORIENTATION THROUGH THE DESTRUCTION OF LOGIC

Television is an "auditory" based medium, according to Schwartz. We react to it the way we react to auditory stimulation, which "envelops" us. McLuhan has characterized television viewing in terms of "all-at-onceness"; that is, the world of syntagm, or orderly and linearly patterned events (and *thinking*) which print fostered, no longer dominates us. As McLuhan wrote in *The Medium is the Massage:*

> The alphabet is a construct of fragmented bits and parts which have no semantic meaning in themselves, and which must be strung together in a line, bead-like and in a prescribed order. Its use fostered and encouraged the habit of perceiving all environment in visual and spatial terms—particularly in terms of a space and a time that are uniform,
>
> c,o,n,t,i,n,u,o,u,s
> and
> c-o-n-n-e-c-t-e-d.
>
> The line, the continuum—this sentence is a prime example—became the organizing principle of life . . . . "Rationality" and logic came to depend on the presentation of connected and sequential facts or concepts.

This "print" world, which created the book and ultimately the factory, fostered individuality, since a "private, fixed point of view became possible." To the extent that logic and fixity are overwhelmed, it can be argued that we find disorientation and, with it, loss of personal identity. All-at-onceness implies all-togetherness, and we are now aware of the way crowds can affect individuals.

Television's very form—its lack of discrete units—contributes to this disorientation. There are no elements to order in a shifting mosaic of partially apprehended dots, so it can be argued that television is, by its nature, illogical as well as disorienting.

McLuhan is not willing to go this far. He says that electronic media (of which television is the most important example) force us into "pattern recognition," as contrasted, say, with logically following an argument. He says, in *The Medium is the Massage:* "We can no longer build serially, block-by-block, step-by-step, because instant communication insures that all factors of the environment and of experience coexist in a state of active interplay." But the instantaneous convergence of "all factors" may produce noise rather than information and lead to paralysis. Pattern recognition is a different way of describing television viewing, but *information which cannot be used logically by people who don't have a fixed point of view is useless.* Television produces terror not by keeping information from us but by overwhelming us with it so that we become disoriented.

HYPERKINESIS: THE "LIBERATION" OF IMPULSE IN SERVICE OF CONTROL

Hyperkinesis is an impulse disorder of children characterized by hyperactivity, irritability, lack of concentration, and poor attention span. There are any number of reasons which have been suggested for it: food additives, parental upbringing, and perhaps television viewing. Whatever its cause or causes, it is a painful affliction for everyone involved: children, parents, schoolmates, etc.

The instantaneity of television, its overpowering immediacy, works toward releasing impulse, which can be defined as "a stimulus that sets the mind in action." Pattern response, from this point of view, is similar to *signal* response. That is, an individual responds not to the meaning of a stimulus but to the stimulus itself, divorced from any social coding which might be involved. I make a distinction here between *signals* and *symbols*. A symbol is something which stands for something else, while a signal has no meaning in itself and merely serves to trigger some kind of response. The bell which set Pavlov's dogs salivating was a signal. The question I ask is whether or not, in more complicated but structurally similar ways, television does the same thing to us?

Sensation, immediacy, envelopment—all these phenomena evade the ego, rationality, and other constraints and produce immediate response. In such a case, can we possibly argue (if, indeed, it is possible to argue anything anymore) that impulsiveness is the same as freedom? Hardly, for impulse here is out of our control. Whoever has a collective tuning fork can strike it and we find ourselves vibrating—though I must admit this situation is not quite as simple as this. The analogy is too simple.

Tony Schwartz uses a better analogy—the responsive chord. Television can be best understood, he says, not as transmitting meaning but in terms of its capacity to generate feedback, what he calls "the resonance principle in communication." He writes:

> Many of our experiences with electronic media are coded and stored in the same way that they are perceived. Since they do not undergo a symbolic transformation, the original experience is more directly available to us when it is recalled. Also, since the experience is not stored in a symbolic form, it cannot be retrieved by symbolic cues. It must be evoked by a stimulus that is coded in the same way as the stored information is coded.

The critical task is to design our package of stimuli so that it resonates with information already stored within an individual and thereby induces the desired learning or behavioral effect. (pp. 24, 25)

We become programmed, so to speak, much the way a computer is programmed. Our experiences are stored in us the way information is stored in a computer, and when the right signal is given, immediately (and in the case of humans, impulsively) the desired behavioral effect is obtained.

DE-INDIVIDUATION THROUGH STANDARDIZATION: PSYCHIC MOBILIZATION

For television to strike responsive chords in the populace at large, it is necessary that there be standardization, to the extent that this is possible. There must be a commonality of information and experience forming what might be called a "culture." America is a multiracial, multiethnic, heterogenous population in one sense, but due to the ubiquity of television and the way it "massages" us all, it can be argued that there are uniformities beneath all the diversity so that we are really a unified and perhaps even standardized people.

The mass media, and particularly television, cut across the economic, social, regional, and religious differences found in American society and provide common experiences while, at the same time, generating and establishing culture codings which imply standardized responses when the chords are sounded.

Although there are many different programs on at any given moment, they all reinforce the *codes*—the secret structures which generate meaning and action in people. The television networks claim they only "give people what they want," but television, as a socializing agent, has created a situation in which often they have been mobilized, psychically, to want what they get. We know that people perceive media selectively, and two-step flow studies show the influence of opinion leaders upon viewers, but despite this, the vastness of the audiences implies standardization and uniformity. This standardization is not of content but of coding. If, for example, individuality is part of the code, it can be shown in any one of a number of different formats—football, drama, games, etc. People who have been psychically mobilized frequently have illusions that they are supreme individualists.

SUMMARY OF SUGGESTED MEDIA EFFECTS

In order to assess the consequences of television, as a medium, upon our sensibilities, let me offer Table 3.1, which brings the above material together and suggests how print and television differ. These phenomena become extremely impoi tant when you consider the sheer volume of television viewing that takes place in America. It is estimated that 96 percent of American homes have television receivers (33 percent have more than one receiver), and the average set is on more than six hours per day. Many children in America watch four to six hours of television each day. It is estimated that by the time an American child reaches high school, he or she will have been exposed to something like 15,000 hours of television, including 650,000 commercials.

Table 3.1: Media Effects

PRINT	EFFECTS	TELEVISION	EFFECTS
Linear	Orientation	Auditory	Disorientation
Logic	Clarity	Pattern Recognition	Confusion
Restraint	Self-Control	Impulse	Hyperkinesis (Conditioning)
Personal, Fixed View	Individualism	Standardization	De-Individuation

The commercials themselves occupy some 3,000 or more *hours,* which means that if a person were to have a job watching commercials 40 hours per week, it would take 75 weeks to view these commercials. And though people do various things while watching television (they go to the bathroom or get snacks during the commercials), the time spent watching television deprives them of time to do other things.

The more we watch television the more we become dissociated from everyday life. We become "abstract" and, despite the information we have, become disoriented. We become cruel perversions of the hero Emerson talked about in *Nature,* a hero who could exclaim, "I become a transparent eyeball; I am nothing. I see all." Television may be affecting our sensorium, and as it becomes unbalanced so will the social order. Ironically, as we find ourselves knowing more and more (or, at least, seeing more and more) we become less and less, until the world, collapsed into the categories listed for us in our weekly *TV Guide,* dematerializes and we become the phantoms Gunther Anders talked about twenty years ago in his essay "The Phantom World of TV." In this essay he writes: "The mass-produced hermit came into being as a new human type, and now millions of them, cut off from each other, yet identical with each other, remain in the seclusion of their homes. Their purpose, however, is not to renounce the world, but to be sure they won't miss the slightest crumb of the world as an image on a screen.'' Tourism is, itself, an important medium, but that is beyond the subject of this paper. But there is an element of compulsion in tourism, whether in real life or in the phantom world, and with it we are not far from terror.

At this point I would like to move on to an examination of the content of television and its consequences. I have neglected the vast and important subject of the rhetoric of the image and the semiology of image analysis, though I will say something about this in my discussion of the relation that exists, in certain situations, between televised images and images in print.

MEDIATED REALITIES ARE NOT ALWAYS TRUTHFUL

For many people, television is considered to be a "window on the world." There is, in this phrase, an assumption that television "shows" you reality and that the camera does not lie. It does not lie but it is selective, so that through its need to focus upon certain things and neglect others, it provides a mediated reality that is not always a truthful one. The situation is analagous to selective perception. The camera may report what it sees but it does not see everything. Frequently what is left out of the field of vision is more important than what is included.

A study of General MacArthur's homecoming in 1951 by Kurt and Gladys Lang (in *Politics and Television*) shows that television's "picture" of the event was considerably different from that of strategically situated observers. Many of the people who viewed the actual event were bored, and the Langs report large numbers of people who said, "We should have stayed home and watched it on TV." MacArthur's appearance in Chicago was not a momentous event and he did not attract large crowds, but the television coverage of this appearance gave a much different picture. The viewers got no sense of "any disappointment or let-down experienced by the crowd," and in addition, because of the extensive use of television close-ups of MacArthur, viewers saw themselves "in a *personal* relationship to the general."

The use of close-ups in fostering an illusory sense of intimacy helped make MacArthur seem much more human and immediate to people, who then found it much easier to empathize with him, especially since his welcome, as portrayed upon television, was so "triumphal."

CYNICISM AND THE ILLUSION OF SELF MASTERY

It has been reported that many people in America, at the age of nine or ten, discover that the commercials which they had trusted previously are full of lies. This leads to cynicism and a strong sense of betrayal. The children then transfer this cynicism from the television commercials to the institutions of society at large, their parents, adults in general, and so on. Cynicism, which the dictionary defines as "contemptuously distrustful of human nature and motives" is a corrosive element which poisons individuals and societies. The children learn, often from experience, to develop defenses which they believe will protect them from being manipulated and exploited.

Sometimes these defenses become so strong that they can never relate to others without fear and anxiety. But their distrust does not prevent them from being manipulated by commercials and programs. Everyone past the age of innocence knows that commercials (even more than programs) distort reality, promise things that their products don't deliver, and cannot be trusted. Nevertheless, we are all affected by these commercials, which play upon our emotions and anxieties. And the illusions we have that we can control ourselves completely make us all the more easily tricked.

As Ernest Dichter, the famous motivation researcher, wrote in his book *The Strategy of Desire:* "Whatever your attitude towards modern psychology or psychoanalysis, it has been proved beyond any doubt that many of our daily decisions are governed by motivations over which we have no control and of which we are often quite aware." The conclusions of a study published in a recent *Harvard Business Review* are ominous: "In most cultures, adolescents have had to deal with social hypocrisy and even with institutionalized lying. But today, TV advertising is stimulating preadolescent children to think about socially accepted hypocrisy. They may be too young to cope with such thought without permanently distorting their views of morality, society and business." It may be argued that it is healthy for children to become aware of the way advertising manipulates them and that advertising is self-defeating (and represents an internal self-contradiction which ultimately will lead to changes in the economics of television and perhaps even society at large). Unfortunately, the fact that advertising is effective even though it is not believed negates this argument, though in the long run the destruction of trust may have its consequences.

VICIOUS CYCLES:
LOSS OF AFFECT AND NARCOTIZATION

I would like to propose model which deals with one of the effects of television viewing and explains why television tends to have such a grip on people. I have noticed that an important theme on television programs, as personified by Mr. Spock of *Star Trek,* is the emotionless man. As I wrote in my book, *The TV-Guided American:*

> As a symbolic hero, he is most significant—he represents the emotional cripple, the mechanical man, the man who has such control of himself and his feelings that he seems to be a robot. As such he represents millions of people who find themselves in the same situation: we are afraid to have emotions; we suppress our feelings because we fear that if we do have feelings we must, inevitably, act on them, and these actions could be destructive.

This notion that Americans are in flight from feelings and emotions was supported by a book by Herbert Hendin, the distinguished psychiatrist, called *The Age of Sensation.* Hendin found that young people now try to live "emotion-free" lives and strive to replace affect with accumulated "fragmented sensory experiences" and drugs (and often both). This, in turn, is having a devastating impact upon family life, which Hendin thinks is in danger of being destroyed by the egocentricity of each member. We must understand egocentricity here to mean emotional self-centeredness as well as selfishness.

But where does television enter into the picture? That link was provided by yet another psychiatrist, Dr. Julius E. Heuscher, in his book, *A Psychiatric Study of Myths and Fairy Tales* (Thomas, 1974). His book is about fairy tales, but he does say something about television and its impact upon young people:

> All through the previous chapters we have seen how folklore stresses the need for a harmonious, gradual human development; how growing up cannot be rushed without serious consequences to the spiritual aspects of the human being. The child who is being presented with an overabundance of adult-life conflicts and desires, and who thereby is being pushed toward grown-up ideas, tends to become afraid of growing up and is therefore stunted in his maturation process (p. 352).

Is it not possible that television causes great difficulties to young people, who shun adult responsibilities, relationships and emotions? We are now ready to see how the vicious cycle in television works:

A. Childhood (and other) television viewing leads to a fear of becoming an adult and being involved in conflicts, emotional relationships, etc.

B. This fear of being an adult leads to an incapacity to have sustained and wholehearted emotional ties and commitments.

C. This incapacity leads to fear of marriage, non-relational sex, fear of feeling (as well as flying), etc.

D. This is not satisfying to those involved, leading to anxiety, pain, and escapism (in drugs and other means, such as television) as a means of obtaining "relief."

E. Television viewing becomes a narcotic upon which we become dependent—to escape from imprisonment within ourselves, have vicarious experiences, know the world (as phantoms), etc. *But at the same time that television programs provide "relief" they also reinforce our childhood fears by* presenting us with characters who do not feel (like Mr. Spock) or conflicting adults (who we do not wish to emulate). It may even be that the fear of being an adult is connected with our notion, given to us to a great degree by television, that adults are "violent."

Thus television, to a great degree, creates the very dependencies which people use it to try to overcome; we become, then, prisoners of our television sets, which leads to our becoming, or remaining, prisoners of ourselves.

THE PRISONER OF PSYCHOLOGY: PRIVATIZATION IN THE CLASSLESS MIDDLE-CLASS SOCIETY

The world of television is a middle-class one. America has a myth of classlessness and sees itself, in its history and on the television tube, as essentially a classless, all-middle-class society. (In a poll I took of my students at San Francisco State University, few students identified themselves as either working-class or upper-class persons; almost all saw themselves as middle class.) There is a kind of fascination with "the poor," who occasionally appear on documentaries and who, in romanticized form, appear on several television shows. But basically the people of television-land are upwardly mobile, self-assertive middle-class types; they are also the heroes of other forms of popular culture, such as love and romance stories in cheap magazines, etc.

As a rule, the characters in television lead private lives; they do not have a social consciousness because, in part, they do not have a conscious ideology. Their goal of "self-realization" involves the consumption of goods, members of the opposite sex, friends, what you will. Erich Fromm describes this as the "marketing orientation," in which one sees the world (and oneself) as a commodity to be marketed or purchased.

The American is what I call a "prisoner of psychology." He can understand psychological phenomena on the basis of his own experience but cannot draw upon this experience to understand social phenomena.

Everything becomes reduced to decisions made by individuals with choices open to them. To the prisoner of psychology, there is no such thing as poverty; there are only poor people. Crime, per se, is only an abstraction, covering a multitude of individual criminal acts. Everything dissolves in the acid of particularism and nominalism, and the politics of the prisoner of psychology is based on the elimination of politics or its negation. Immersed in the prison of himself, the prisoner of psychology will tolerate no extraneous considerations.

This represents a kind of naive optimism which is typical of the petty bourgeois mentality. Arnold Hauser describes how it is reflected in the cinema, but the situation is analagous for television. He says in *The Social History of Art:*

> It [the middle class] has always felt menaced from above and below, but has preferred to give up its real interests rather than its hopes and alleged prospects. It has wanted to be reckoned as part of the bourgeois upper class, although in reality it shared the lot of the lower class. But without a clear-cut and clarified social position no coherent consciousness and consistent outlook on life is possible, and the film producer has been able to rely quite safely on the disorientation of these rootless elements of society. The petty bourgeois attitude is typified by a thoughtless, uncritical optimism. It believes in the ultimate unimportance of social differences and, accordingly, wants to see films in which people walk out of one social stratum into another. For this middle class the cinema gives fulfillment to the social romanticism which life never realizes. . . (Vol. 4, p. 253).

The final result of all this is alienation and loneliness which make the narcissistic fantasies produced by television more necessary and more bitter.

VIOLENCE

Much has been written about the all-pervasive violence on American television. Because of the various complexities involved in studying human behavior, social scientists have had a great deal of trouble in demonstrating, conclusively, that anything causes anything else. The report to the surgeon general entitled *Television and Growing Up: The Impact of Televised Violence* deals with this problem of complexity as follows: "The impact of televised violence on the viewers, as a reading of this report will show, is embedded in a complicated set of related variables." Nevertheless, the report did come to the conclusion that ". . . a modest relationship exists between the viewing of violence on television and aggressive tendencies." There was a great deal of controversy about the members of the committee that wrote the report and organized the studies; it seems that the television networks were able to eliminate some of the most critical scholars, thus guaranteeing that a strong condemnation of television would not be forthcoming.

Violence is a form of self-assertiveness and aggressiveness, and like most aggression is connected to frustration. Some theorists have suggested that violence is caused, in large measure, by sexual frustration and other matters connected with sexuality. Thus, sexual repression is the subliminal trigger which sets off much of the violence found in our society and on our television tubes. I cannot deal with the subject of violence adequately here, in this prospectus, but its ubiquity suggests it is intimately connected with our social structure and is an indicator of profound malaise.

POSSIBILITARIANISM

In *The Man Without Qualities,* Robert Musil has a chapter titled "If There is Such A Thing as Reality, There Must Also Be a Sense of Possibility." He defines *possibilitarianism* as the capacity to think that something "could probably just as easily be some other way," and mentions that when this is found in children it is "vigorously driven out of them, and in their presence such people are referred to as crackbrains, dreamers, weaklings, know-alls, carpers and cavillers." People who cannot, for one reason or another, summon up any "realities" about themselves have no qualities then—setting the stage for the development of the new hero (or antihero), the man without qualities.

It is television more than any other medium, I believe, that destroys our sense of possibility and creates terror. Television provides collective fantasies and daydreams, and these mass-produced fantasies have a tendency to get in the way of our private ones. Television attacks our rationality, turns us into creatures of whim and impulse, and standardizes our experience to such an extent that our individuality is crushed, though we are given the illusion that we are autonomous and free. Television distorts our sense of reality—if it is a mirror, it is a distorting one. It breeds cynicism in the young and attacks their capacity to have emotionally satisfying, permanent relationships. It projects a world of middle-class people who find happiness in consuming an endless supply of products, who have fantasies of moving out of their social situation when they feel like it, and who are so self-absorbed that they are almost autistic.

Television is the great instrument of what Hans Magnus Enzenberger calls "the consciousness industry," whose basic purpose is to sell the existing order. He writes in "The Industrialization of the Mind":

> All of us, no matter how irresolute we are, like to think that we reign supreme in our own consciousness, that we are masters of what our minds accept or reject. Since the Soul is not much mentioned any more, except by priests, poets, and pop musicians, the last refuge a man can take from the catastrophic world at large seems to be his own mind. Where else can he expect to withstand the daily siege, if not within himself? Even under the conditions of totalitarian rule, where no one can fancy any more that his home is his castle, the mind of the individual is considered a kind of last citadel and hotly defended, though this imaginary fortress may have been long since taken over by an ingenious enemy.
>
> No illusion is more stubbornly upheld than the sovereignty of the mind. It is a good example of the impact of philosophy on people who ignore it; for the idea that men can "make up their minds" individually and by themselves is essentially derived from the tenets of bourgeois philosophy: secondhand Descartes, rundown Husserl, armchair idealism; and all it amounts to is a sort of metaphysical do-it-yourself.

Enzenberger and others have argued that there are certain contradictions found in capitalist countries (and other societies) which will lead to a change in media and that the "manipulation" theory of media is archaic. He believes that only "a free socialist society will be able to make them [the media] fully productive."

At this moment in time, it is still possible to see television as an instrument of terror. "Compulsion and the illusion of freedom converge," as Henri LeFebvre wrote in *Everyday Life in the Modern World;* and "unacknowledged compulsions" shape and organize our lives. Television, more than any other medium, has created the man with commodities who is without qualities. It has robbed us of our sense of possibility and our sense of reality. This need not be the case, and perhaps someday it won't be. That is a possibility which I hope will be a reality.

BIBLIOGRAPHY

Barthes, Roland. *Mythologies.* New York: Hill & Wang, 1972.
_____. "Rhetoric of the Image." *Working Papers,* Spring 1971.
Berger, Arthur Asa. *Li'l Abner: A Study in American Satire.* New York: Twayne, 1970.
_____. *Pop Culture.* Dayton, Ohio: Pflaum/Standard, 1973.

_____. *About Man: An Introduction to Anthropology.* Dayton, Ohio: Pflaum/Standard, 1974.

_____. *The Comic-Stripped American.* New York: Walker, 1974.

_____. *The TV-Guided American.* New York: Walker, 1976.

_____. "Politics of the Comics." *Crimmer's,* Spring 1976.

_____. "The Six Million Dollar Man." *Society,* July/Aug. 1976.

_____. "Unflattering Definitions: Stereotypes of Americans in the Comics," 1976 (mimeo).

_____, ed. *Film in Society.* New Brunswick, N.J.: Transaction, 1979.

Eco, Umberto. "Towards a Semiotic Inquiry into the Television Message." *Cultural Studies,* Autumn 1972.

Enzenberger, Hans M. *The Consciousness Industry.* New York: Seabury Press, 1974.

Lang, Kurt, and Gladys Lang. *Politics and Television.* Chicago: Quadrangle, 1968.

McLuhan, Marshall. *Understanding Media.* New York: McGraw-Hill, 1964.

_____. *The Medium Is the Massage.* New York: Bantam, 1967.

Schwartz, Tony. *The Responsive Chord.* New York: Anchor, 1974.

The Last Word

(Television Columns from *Focus* magazine)

THE CULTURAL CONSEQUENCES OF THE COMMERCIAL

Sometimes It Only Takes 30 Seconds

Although it may seem strange to spend time dealing with "interruptions" in programs (which is one way of looking at commercials), the fact is that these seemingly minor irritations are an important part of a thirty-billion-dollar industry—advertising—which has considerable effect on our media, our society, and our psyches. We spend almost half as much money on advertising as we do on our entire educational system, and the extracurricular education we get from advertising—and commercials in particular—must not be underestimated.

After all, if you think about it, commercials exist for one purpose—to shape our behavior. They are extremely expensive to produce and to broadcast. A half-minute commercial can cost $100,000 to make and $50,000 to run on a popular program. For *one* half-minute that is. . . if you run that commercial twenty times, you've spend a million dollars just for air time.

Now it is impossible to say that commercials and commercials alone are the sole agents which are responsible for the things I'm going to talk about. I can't prove everything, but you decide for yourself whether there's logic to my argument. Obviously the companies which sponsor commercials think they are getting some kind of payoff (such as more customers, increased sales), otherwise they wouldn't spend millions of dollars for advertising campaigns. The question is whether these commercials have other effects, side-effects, which might not even have been intended by the agencies which made the commercials.

The first topic I would like to talk about is the matter of *cynicism*. Young people who watch television commercials learn, at a relatively early age, that they cannot trust commercials. From this they conclude that they cannot trust adults in general, and they become very cynical about government, society, and our institutions. A recent study published in the *Harvard Business Review* documents this. It suggests that children become "self-protective" and that this tends to "... make them defensive and distrustful of society."

I would add that although children, and adults, recognize that commercials are full of exaggerations and lies, this knowledge does not protect them from being manipulated. The average viewer has the illusion that he can prevent himself from being swayed. He does not recognize that commercials touch responsive chords deep in his unconscious and give subliminal messages which evade his consciousness.

Point two. I believe there is a relationship that exists between over-the-counter drug commercials and drug abuse. I don't think that drug advertising is the only cause of drug abuse, but I think it is a contributory cause. These commercials supply models which gave us a notion of how the world works and how to maneuver within it. The basic model we get from drug commercials is what I call the "Pain-Pill-Pleasure" model. Problems are solved by taking magic pills. There is a "better life through chemistry." We all are plagued by all kinds of problems—aching back, tension, nausea, headache, etc.—but in all cases, we are told, there is some thing which can be purchased which will take care of any particular problem. It is not much of a leap from the notion that small problems can be taken care of by taking legal drugs and remedies to the notion that big problems can be "fixed" by taking narcotics.

We are exposed to the "Pain-Pill-Pleasure" model so often that it is deeply ingrained in our psyches. It is certainly part of our behavior, since statistics show that America is a pill-popping nation, with countless number of pill junkies of one sort or another.

The Federal Trade Commission is now investigating drug commercials and trying to determine whether it can be shown that commercials do, in fact, contribute to drug abuse. A few years ago it would have seemed quite a far fetched notion.

Manufacturers and advertisers usually defend themselves by arguing "we're only giving the people what they want." This is not exactly the case, however, for what people want has already been, to a large degree, shaped by the media in its function as a socializing agent. What people want is often what they've been taught to want and made to want.

Sometimes it only takes thirty seconds.

LA FORMATION
(La Science et L'Image)

Early in September, I received a letter from the Centre National de la Recherche Scientifique inviting me to participate in a conference they were sponsoring on "Science and the Image," which was to be held in

Thonon, a lovely little French town near Geneva. The conference was being run by a branch of the CNRS (pronounced in French it is "Say-Enh-Err-Ess") with the unwieldy and cumbersome title "service d'etude, de realisation et de diffusion de documents audio-visuels" whose initials spell SERDDAV. The French love acronyms and have created a seemingly infinite number of them for their various organizations. Thus, in addition to the CNRS's SERDDAV, there were people from INA—the Institut National de L'Audiovisuel, and a number of other acronymized entities.

The point of all this is to emphasize one thing—the French are vitally concerned with audio-visual education, with media of all sorts, and with the effect that film and television have upon society. The subtitle of the conference was "the moving image," and it was because of the work that I had done with television that I was invited.

For my presentation, I expanded the first article I had written for this column, "Television as an Instrument of Terror," into a much longer essay, which I sent on ahead of me. I also sent a telegram accepting the invitation and a letter asking for details. What I did not know was that because of difficulties in the mailroom at San Francisco State University, letters were being delayed from ten days to two weeks. So though I received my tickets, I never received a letter telling me where in Thonon I was to go, what arrangements had been made for me, or anything of that nature, because they had not received my letter, I imagine.

In any case, I knew that there was a conference in Thonon and I had a ticket which would get me there, so I assumed it would not be too hard to find out where the conference was being held. It is a strange feeling, I must say, to travel 8,000 miles and not know where, exactly, you are to go and what, specifically, you are to do. I arrived in Thonon about noon, October 2, and found the town covered with posters announcing the conference. I proceeded then to the Art and Culture Center, where it was being held, and found it swarming with people who had come from all over the world to show films, to talk about media, to present ideas about the media, and so on. I found that a hotel room had been reserved for me, and before long discovered myself surrounded by extremely amiable and animated people, all of whom had an enormous amount to say about science, images, and society (and most of whom were wearing bluejeans).

I was to spend the next six days, from morning to night, immersed in media talk. There was talk about techniques, and we had presentations by Jean Pierre Beauviala, inventor of the Aaton camera, and Stephane Kudelski, the audio engineer who makes the remarkable Nagra tape recorders. There was a battle royal between the filmmakers who favored 16mm film cameras and those who favored the Super-8. The phrase "Super-huit" was to be heard echoing in the conference room over and over again; its proponents argued it would help create the "revolution." One television critic bulldozed the convention into watching an hour-long videotape he had made with a minicamera invented by Beauviala, and then discussed it for two hours, explaining that his tape would lead to "the revolution." (Many held that his tape was a grand example of narcissism and that the evening was good psychodrama, but not in any way revolutionary.)

The French have a wonderful word, *formation,* which is similar to our term "socialization" but somewhat different. They are concerned with the role television plays in the *formation* of French youth; the connotations of the word are what is interesting. *Formation* is much more concrete, suggests something more direct and personal. How do people arrive at themselves? How are they *formed?* (I was asked about my own *formation.* In this case it meant, "Where and what did you study?")

It occurred to me that the word *formation* is to be found in the word "information," which suggests that information has a much stronger role than we might imagine, as far as our development is concerned. I have seen statistics which claim that the average person in America spends something like five hours a *year* reading books and 1,200 hours a year watching television. If this is the case, it is the images on television, more than almost anything else, which are responsible for our *formation.* Or is it *deformation?*

COLLECTIVE DAYDREAMS

Television programs have been characterized by some students of media as "collective daydreams"—projections of the desires, fantasies, hopes, and dreams of the American public, filtrates of the consciousness of writers and producers. The television industry argues that it is only giving people what they want—and what the American television public seems to want, more and more, are violence and other potentially destructive kinds of programming. But it's only entertainment, we are told. . . so don't go around making a mountain out of a murder, or three.

The television industry can show you stacks of statistics which show that people are satisfied with what they are getting, and a look at the listing of most popular programs of any week is enough to scare anyone with aspirations toward "uplifting" the taste levels of the masses. Or with faith in the ability of the general public to select so-called "good" programs. (We can always ask ourselves, "Good for what?")

The reason daydreams, even commercially created ones, are important is that they give us insights into what people are really concerned with, and how they see themselves—which often cannot be found out by opinion polls and that sort of thing.

In the introduction to a fascinating book, *Psychoanalysis and Social Research,* psychiatrist Herbert Hendin and his colleagues point out that individuals are "not consciously aware of most of the significant attitudes and dynamic patterns shaping their thinking and behavior." Hendin suggests that the psychiatric interview, based on free associations, dreams, fantasies, etc., is more useful than traditional techniques because it circumvents the defenses which people (often unconsciously) construct. The person being interviewed, we are told, "often reveals his inner feelings unawares."

Hendin then discusses some research he conducted in Norway and compares his findings with those of a sociologist who "accepted at face value statements by Norwegian women that in their country the woman plays a completely submissive role in marriage." What Hendin discovered, when he got Norwegian women to talk freely, discuss their dreams, etc., was that they saw themselves as stronger than their husbands, that their mothers had dominated their fathers, and that the women were the more effective figures in most of their friends' marriages. These Norwegian women dreamed of their husbands as children and babies. When pressed to explain the discrepancy between their statements and their dreams, the women admitted that "women are stronger than men, but a man must be allowed to think he is stronger."

What all this means is that we have to be careful about accepting people's answers to questionnaires or the typical question-and-answer interview. People have a tendency to give the answers they think they are expected to, or to give answers they themselves want to believe. People often don't reveal their true feelings.

Given this problem, is it not sensible to avoid those "rehearsed responses" and instead examine people's fantasies—or, in the case of television, the fantasies they find interesting and compelling? If a program is popular, it must, in some way, take care of viewers' needs and give them rewards and gratifications of one sort or another. It is not enough to say that a program is popular because it is full of gratuitous violence or is moronic or submoronic and therefore appeals to the mythical lowest common denominator. It is not terribly rewarding to deal with aesthetic matters alone—for most commercial programs are formula-written hack work. Even so, they may deal with themes of compelling significance to the viewing public. They may reveal trends, attitudes, values, beliefs, etc. among the audience that are not made evident by other means.

When we look upon television programs not so much as programs but as collective daydreams (and, at times, collective nightmares), they take on a much more profound significance. The heroes and heroines take on a symbolic dimension of considerable importance, and the subjects, themes, structures of the programs, and resolutions (to mention only a few topics) demand our attention and interpretation. These collective daydreams contain hidden ideologies—a hidden curriculum—affecting our feelings and behavior.

And yet, curiously enough, except for the work of some critics and media scholars, most people are blind to the power and effects of television programs. Their illusions about the sovereignty of their minds and their control of themselves make them all the more susceptible to the collective daydreams upon which they feed.

SCOPOPHILIA AND THE NEW IMAGE
OF WOMEN ON TELEVISION

The most popular television program of recent months is *Charlies's Angels*—a detective series featuring three beautiful young women who fight crime. Having *three* women is a quantum leap in programming sophistication. Before, there was just one—*The Bionic Woman*—which used to be the most popular program. As every Peeping Tom knows, when it comes to voyeurism, three women are better than one.

As I write this I must imagine that in New York or Los Angeles, wherever such decisions are made, plans are under way to have a program with four, five, seven, or nine beautiful women who will fight crime, often while scantily attired. The logic is inescapable. Also, having more lithe bodies to lust after enables better possibilities: I can envision a whole army of beautiful women, a veritable collection of Miss Universes from every country, catering to every taste in lust and leering.

In a recent adventure on *Charlie's Angels,* one of the heroines worked at an imitation Playboy Club, and this naturally meant she had to pour herself into one of those revealing waitress costumes. For the future, the possibilities are endless. I can see murders taking place in nudist colonies or topless bars, involving satanic cults, makers of blue movies, etc.

All of this smells of the rankest kind of sexploitation, and it is. Most of our popular arts have found ways to exhibit almost every portion of woman's (and in some cases man's) anatomy to all the *scopophiliacs* around. Scopophilia, for those of you not up on psychiatry, is defined in Hinsie's *Psychiatric Dictionary* as "sexual pleasure derived from contemplation or looking." (Our elite arts are no different, though the ambience of refinement makes us feel better about our voyeurism.) Until someone developed the concept of a team of beautiful women detectives, it was becoming more difficult to find pretexts for displaying sartorially compromised women. This is no longer the case.

But something else is being revealed in these programs. These women are both beautiful and *punishing*. They are, after all, avengers of injustice and sometimes, as in the case of the Bionic Woman, Jaime (*J'aime,* I love) Sommers, they are infinitely more powerful than the typical male.

TV superwomen are not always physically stronger. In some cases they are emotionally and psychologically more powerful, as in *The Nancy Walker Show.* Here we have a pint-sized dynamo married to an ineffectual husband. The *menage* is completed by her effeminate male secretary who twitters around with limp wrists.

Nancy is a threatrical agent, which explains the presence of beautiful models and actresses—her clients—who are forever trying out for commercials or roles in sitcoms. This allows them to display their bodies in suggestive poses while Nancy bargains for contracts and resolves the women's predicaments.

The leading figures in many current situation comedies are women: Maude, Rhoda, Mary Tyler Moore, and Phyllis are probably the best examples. In some cases they may be silly, but in most cases they are dominant figures.

A good case can be made, I would argue, that women are being shown in a new light. There is a new image of women on television which is most interesting—they are often attractive and hence a potential source of love and gratification for men, but they are also powerful and in some cases punishing. This makes me wonder whether, underneath it all, these television programs reveal a male subliminal fear of female sexual potency. Could it be that men exploit women and treat them as sexual objects because they are afraid of them? What seems to be a casualness about women in many male roles is permeated by a deep-seated fear that they will use their bodies to manipulate or deceive men and eventually, when they get the chance, they will punish men.

I read, recently, about a lecture a psychiatrist gave on "passive men and wild, wild women," which argued that men are becoming increasingly "inactive, withdrawn and silent at home," and that this passivity is driving women crazy. I would imagine that men have always had ambivalent feelings about women. The story of Adam and Eve blames woman for Adam's fall, and an early church father said, if I recall correctly, that "a woman is a temple over a sewer." But I wonder whether the negative part of the ambivalence has been modified somewhat—from hostility to fear—while the positive part has been transformed from desire into voyeurism and scopophilia?

EROS AND (AG)APE

King Kong, the original 1933 *King Kong* that is, was shown on television recently—competing with the second installment of *Roots.* I felt duty-bound to watch *Roots,* a production which I found rather heavy-handed and overdone, though the subject is, admittedly, an important one. It is one that is worthy of better treatment, as a matter of fact, and many critics have suggested that the series carried on public broadcasting is more accurate and more sensitively done.

I was watching on the channel which broadcast *King Kong* when it started, and just before I switched to *Roots.* I saw the great ape towering on the landscape and wondered about the strange feeling that came over me as I watched King Kong roaring away.

What is there about apes that fascinates us so much. And why do we often, in films and other forms of popular culture, pair apes with ladies? At this moment two versions of *King Kong* exist—the original, made in 1933, and a more modern and less exciting one (so I've heard) that has recently appeared. I understand that yet a third *King Kong* is being planned. In addition, there are countless jungle films which have episodes involving apes and ladies, including one spectacular Tarzan film which has a really exciting scene in which he rescues a terrified damsel from the clutches of a gigantic (for the times—he was only about ten feet tall) ape. If I recall correctly, the huge ape was a kind of "god" for the pygmy tribe which held the ape captive and worshipped it, at the same time.

We know that apes are, in fact, timid creatures, despite their gargantuan size. It is not possible that we project our violent feelings onto these poor creatures, who become our "rivals" for the beautiful women they become paired with?

Can apes love women—as we know the word love? There are, it seems, two kinds of love—eros and agape. Eros was the god of love in Greek mythology, and erotic love, love which is strongly affected by sexual desire, is the kind of love we are most familiar with in movies and in television programs. But there is another king of love, agape, which we encounter from time to time—in saints and heroes and all those who have unselfish love that does not have sexual connotations.

Film historians who have analyzed *King Kong* and examined material cut from the film assure us that King Kong's love was erotic, though we would imagine it would be agape that he (or should we say "it") felt. Perhaps this insight explains the resonance that *King Kong* has (and all the other ape/maiden stories).

Obviously, there is more to the ape/maiden business than meets the eye. Otherwise, how do you explain the power *King Kong* has? How do you explain the film's capacity to capture our imagination and make us feel deeply about the fate of this gargantuan ape? Thy situation is an absurd one, and yet we are moved.

This is so because, strangely enough, King Kong's story is our story. Let me explain.

What I am suggesting here is that there is an Oedipal component to these stories. Think, for example, of the relationships we find. A bad ape (good apes don't bother with women, so we presume) has this desirable female, and a jungle hero must fight the ape to rescue the maiden. This can be shown graphically, and expanded upon, as follows:

Man	Ape
Son	Father
Humanity	Animality
Society	Nature
Tarzan	*King Kong*

These are the two polarities, and in between, mediating between them, is the lady.

While it might seem rather strange to equate apes, and King Kong in particular, with "fathers," we must realize we are dealing with collective dreams in which there is a great deal of disguise and symbolization. The case becomes stronger when you realize that the king figure grows out of the father figure, and that in some languages the word for king is the same (or similar to) that for father. In his essay, "The Myth of the Birth of the Hero," Otto Rank says that we find "the use of identical words for king and father, in the Indo-Germanic languages (compare the German *Landesvater,* "father of his country"—king)."

Gradually we separated the king figure from the father figure, but psychologically speaking, the two are joined together. We then displace our fathers onto King Kong, if I am correct—a figure we can show our hostility towards (by shooting him off the Empire State building or some other phallic edifice) with little fear of being punished.

There is a famous cartoon by Charles Addams which shows a huge ape carrying off a lovely young maiden. A woman, sitting on the veranda of a cottage on the fringe of the jungle, says to a friend, "I wonder what he sees in her?" It is a question we may all wonder about—though for reasons more ponderous than we might imagine?

THE QUINTESSENCE OF PYTHONISM

Monty Python is one of the most popular programs broadcast on public television, a series which has legions of devotees who follow it with an almost religious zeal. I find it often amusing, generally clever, and at times brilliant—but there is something about the program that bothers me. Perhaps it is because when I was living in England, a few years back, I heard such raves about the program that I anticipated something so remarkable that *Monty Python,* or any program for that matter, would have left me unsatisfied. Thus my expectations may have something to do with my feelings about the program. But I think there is something else.

I am also somewhat puzzled by its popularity in America since, as a rule, British television comedians such as Benny Hill, Morecambe and Wise, Ronnie Corbett, etc. are virtually unknown in America. It is doubtful that the typical British video comedy would be appreciated in America, for we are much too sophisticated, as a rule, for British "piss-tit" humor. British video humor tends to be much cruder and raunchier than American comedy, which is much more middle-class in its ambience.

What most Americans like about *Monty Python* is its anarchism— everything from the Church of England to sports to sex is grist for its comic militancy. All the stereotypes we have are mercilessly destroyed by being held up for observation, exaggerated, and savagely ridiculed. In any given half-hour, a number of the major institutions of the civilized world (as well as some of our most important private fantasies) are often satirized and spoofed, frequently in very inventive ways.

The group is well named, for like pythons they seem to squeeze the life out of anyone or anything they are able to coil themselves around. They are especially good at deflating the pompous, as well as showing the mean, pathetic, and nasty qualities of the common man. Each program is very fast-paced, and we are distracted, then, from the fact that a vast constriction is going on. While we watch zany clerics from the Church of England, weird constables, eccentric military officers, shrewish wives, screwball aristocrats, and maniacal civil servants (to name just a small number of their creations), the python is winding itself around us until we find ourselves completely entangled.

What is this pythonism I'm talking about? What is the quintessence of pythonism? As I see it, pythonism is a comedic nihilism, mixed with touches of elitism, that is ultimately not liberating but depressing. American humor tends to be equalitarian—we are antiauthoritarian and take great delight in spoofing those with pretensions, those who have illusions about themselves, anyone who makes a claim to being better than anyone else, or anyone who has power over others.

In *Monty Python,* however, I find that there is little sympathy for the common man, and though, in many cases, he is a comic or even pathetic character, you get no sense of compassion or feeling for him, or anyone else. I can think of few sympathetic characters in any of the sketches; instead, what we find is a collection of grotesques (which is shown graphically in the animated sections), or comic creations who seem devoid of humanity, who are basically one-dimensional. So when we laugh at the skits and jokes, it is not because we have learned something about the human condition and about the absurdities and wonders of life, but rather it is a kind of scornful, hostile, nasty laughing we do.

All this, of course, is personal opinion. Many people do not take humor seriously; doing so seems to be a contradiction in terms. And yet, curiously enough, the greatest minds in history have spent an enormous amount of intellectual energy trying to find out why we laugh and what significance humor has for the psyche and society.

At its best humor is wonderfully liberating—it frees us from bondage to conventions, it lifts our repressions, it helps us deal with guilt, and it suggests, always, that things might be different. Jokes, if you think about it, are full of surprises, and punch lines tell us that we can't be certain what is coming next and that we must always be ready for surprises. Humor tells us that the patterns we find in our lives have no inner necessity and that a great deal in life is arbitrary and the result of chance, which means there is always hope. Good humor is entertaining and great humor is life-affirming.

Monty Python, though often clever (and often silly and inane), leaves a sour taste in my mouth, alas. *Ex nihilo nihil fit;* out of nothing, nothing comes.

A MODEST PROPOSAL

Readers of this column are probably used to finding me in a state of excitation (defined as "the irritability induced in protoplasm by a stimulus") over the *content* of television. Although there is a good deal on television that is admirable, I have tended, I confess, to focus my attention on topics that I found disturbing. But let me leave off beating a dead horse and move now to a related topic, the matter of programming.

And what do we find when we look at television programming—that is, the structure of programming found on the different channels during the week—what do we find? *Anarchy.* An examination of the daily television log reveals that at any given moment in the day, with few exceptions, there is a chaos of different kinds of programs. (This is especially true of the most critical hours, the evening hours after seven.)

A person interested in a good undiluted evening of murder, for example, has to switch from this channel to that one, and frequently to still a third and sometimes even a fourth or fifth channel before his bloodlust is sated. The same applies to other kinds of programs, too. Except for a rare occasion, such as Thanksgiving or New Years day, it is impossible to watch more than two or three football games in one day on any one channel.

Why is this so?

Because network executives are basically conservative people who have been socialized to run television the way it has always been run, which is to have a string of different programs following one after the other. Sometimes you can get a few situation comedies that have been strung together, or game shows or detective shows, but for the most part, if you think of it, you never can be sure what will be on.

Now the term radical means *root,* and radicals are people who want to improve societies or institutions by going to their roots and restructuring them. The important term here is structure; you have to restructure if you want to do anything more than make cosmetic (superficial) changes. How would this work in terms of the television schedule? The answer is so simple it is simply amazing it hasn't been tried on television before.

If you think about it, there are just a few genres or program types which are shown on television. Television, remember, is just a medium which carries various kinds of programs such as news shows, sports programs, commercials, and so on. There are, it turns out, a dozen basic genres, which I list below:

News and documentaries	Humor (including sitcoms)
Commercials	Soap operas
Sports	Love and sex
Game shows	Food preparation
Culture	Variety shows
Crime shows	Movies

These twelve program genres are the most important kinds of television shows and each deserves its own channel. My proposal then is to restructure television so that a given channel carries nothing but one kind of program. The advantages of this structural rearrangement are numerous.

First, various kinds of program "freaks" can simply turn on the tube and never have to worry about getting up to switch channels. Since all commercials will be on one channel, none of the programs will be interrupted, though adequate time will be left at the end of each program for people to have a snack or go to the bathroom.

Second, viewers will be able to have "in-depth" experiences. Poor people can watch gourmet cooks all day long and vicariously enjoy the finest fare. People who lack love can watch romance for an entire evening on the love and sex channel and have their fill of blondes, brunettes, Samsons, and other studs. And if you are feeling blue, you can be certain of a whole evening of comedy on the humor channel. Or you might get good therapeutic advice on the "culture" channel. That channel will be devoted to the arts, and each evening will have ballet, opera, lectures by learned savants, panels of professors, and that kind of thing.

Third, The Berger Plan avoids silly duplication. Frequently we find two or even three of the same kind of program are on at the same time, which means that we have to miss one or two of them. This will no longer be the case. People with a passion for soap operas, for instance, will be able to watch every one, if they care to. No longer will they suffer from anxiety as they are torn between competing programs, no longer will they know the pangs of soporific deprivation.

There are, no doubt, some cranks who will fail to see the sublime simplicity and logic of my modest proposal. They will argue that there are more than just twelve kinds of programs carried on television. My answer to them is this—if so, we could have these programs carried on the variety channel or we could carry them on UHF. But what, you may ask, about a program that has, say, a humorous detective or a psychopathic killer who laughs hysterically all the time? *Which* channel does that go on? Or what about a hysterically laughing psychopathic killer who is also a sex maniac? Which of the three possible channels might that program be carried on? That is a relatively trivial problem which can be solved by a flip of the coin or by establishing some panel which is empowered to decide such things.

You may be somewhat shocked by this modest proposal, but think of the difference it might make in our television viewing. Radio has already moved in the direction I've been discussing. Can television be far behind?

The Six Million Dollar Man

What are we to make of *The Six Million Dollar Man?* The program is frequently corny and melodramatic, and most of the actors in it are refugees from grade B films. The acting is often flat and mechanical, as if the technological premise of the program affected the actors. It is a sloppily produced, inept program at times, though occasionally it is beautifully realized.

In a recent episode, "Divided Loyalty," only Lee Majors—the lead actor—gave a creditable performance. The story was pure soap opera: it involved a brilliant scientist (all scientists are "brilliant" in SMDM-land, and many are deranged) who had defected to a Communist-dominated Eastern European country but who now wanted to return to America because he did not want his son to grow up in a totalitarian society. Thus he was willing to risk his life and a prison term in America to escape to "freedom." Steve Austin (Majors) was sent to help him in this enterprise.

The situation was complicated by the fact that the son did not get along with his father who—for many years—had been totally absorbed in his work and neglected him. Sounds familiar! To complicate matters further, the son had become friends with a guard, Boris, who was a stepfather to him. Thus the son had divided loyalty and was caught between his real father and his "adopted" father, Boris: the boy's mother had conveniently died at childbirth.

This situation could easily have been something out of *Mission Impossible,* and the episode had touches of the *Mission Impossible* formula: the use of photographs of the characters while a voice (not on a tape recorder in this instance) explained the situation and sent Steve Austin off on his dangerous mission. Being a Six Million Dollar Man, Austin can do what the whole *Mission Impossible* team did; so although he cost a great deal of money, he is relatively inexpensive. With the Six Million Dollar Man, as with most other military hardware, the initial price is steep. But in the long run your money gives a good return.

The boy creates obstacles—he punctures the radiator of a jeep which was to be used in the escape and inadvertently causes his father to become blind (though this blindness is only temporary). Finally, after numerous heroics and only a few violent scenes (sometimes shown in slow motion, as in *Kung Fu*), Austin manages to lead the scientist and his son to safety. At one point, still blind and thinking that he will remain so and will also be captured by the police, the father confesses to his son that he loves him and begs forgiveness; the boy then "makes up" with the father.

In the end, of course, the father is pardoned. He was, in effect, a double traitor—thus the negation of the negation adds up to heroism in this program's perverse logic. Steve Austin also finds a moment to tell the boy that in America he can be anything he wants to be if he works hard enough. Thus the story ends on a happy note of reconciliation and optimism. So much for a typical episode blending—in this case—nineteenth-century political economics and twentieth-century medical technology.

The episode described here was so sentimental and cliché ridden (though it may have been a particularly bad example) that it is impossible to believe that the program's popularity rests on the adventures themselves. Why was this program at one time the most popular one for American adults in the 18-45 age group?

The show's popularity rests on the significance of the Six Million Dollar Man as a heroic figure, a half-machine, half-man "person-thing" who transcends the stupid adventures in which he is involved. There is a mythic dimension to the Six Million Dollar Man which speaks to the needs of and sounds a responsive chord in the psyches of many of the people watching him (including children, too, who are avid followers of the program). He is a cultural hero worth considering.

The most interesting point about Steve Austin (and the name suggests both Hercules and Texas) is that he is part machine; he represents a fusion between living flesh and machine technology, and where one begins and the other ends is an enigma. The story of his creation and re-creation is told at the start of every episode.

A rocket malfunctions and its astronaut-pilot, Steve Austin, is saved. He has lost one eye and various parts of his body. In the operation in which he is "fixed," a voice says, "We can make you better"—an absurd proposition, but a fine example of technological hubris.

Austin emerges from this operation a superhuman individual with telescopic vision and enormous strength who can run seventy miles per hour and leap great heights. He is still vulnerable and can be gassed, knocked unconscious, and so forth, but his great strength makes it impossible for his enemies to triumph over him.

This matter of grafting machines onto man (or vice versa) is of considerable importance, and work is being done now to help people who have lost limbs lead normal lives. Eventually, scientists tell us, machine-man symbiosis will be realized. Steve Austin, a "living doll," is an indication of things to come.

In the future, scientists will make us all "better," which will only mean that the level of power and violence will be turned up still another notch, and we will all be equal once more—except that we will all have an even harder punch.

That Austin is a strong male is of consequence; he represents an ego-ideal for millions of youngsters who were duped by the campy Batman and who do not have many powerful males on television to emulate outside of characters on the police force. It is worth pointing out that the Six Million Dollar Man figure (doll) is one of the most successful "male dolls" ever made. This doll is acceptable to fathers who ordinarily do not let their sons play with dolls, fearing that they will become homosexuals. Steve Austin in not a homosexual, though he does not have a sex life.

The violence in the program is contained in a few incidents; there is a finality and unreality about it that diminishes its impact. Feats of strength replace physical combat as an indicator of virility and power. Obviously there is no contest when the Six Million Dollar Man fights an ordinary human, though at times other extremely powerful figures are created to battle with him.

On the other hand, Austin's power emphasizes the weakness and powerlessness of the ordinary man. The more the Six Million Dollar Man performs prodigies—the more he uproots trees, carries enormous weights, rips open boxcars as if they were cereal boxes—the more we recognize our pettiness and weakness. The Six Million Dollar Man is a humanly created superhuman figure, and his strength makes us conscious of our frailty and deals our already weakened psyches yet another blow.

Like the superlative, the superhero creates, as Leo Lowenthal wrote, "a reign of psychic terror where the masses have to realize the pettiness and insignificance of their everyday life. The already weakened consciousness of being an individual is struck another heavy blow by the pseudo-individualizing forces of the superlative"—and, we can add, by the superhuman.

Thus while Austin is a strong male figure—and we need all of these figures we can find—his superhuman power has certain negative consequences for his followers. Unlike a hero such as Superman, who was born on a foreign planet, the Six Million Dollar Man is an ordinary human who was *made powerful* by doctors and scientists. In many respects, he is a figure from the comics, and he represents a dream we all have: that new developments in science will help us become powerful and, ultimately, immortal.

This lust for immortality, buried deep within our psyches and dealt with in every program when we see the Six Million Dollar Man being "created," is the key to the program's popularity. Steve Austin holds the possibility of escaping the grim reaper (who presumably cannot run seventy miles an hour or leap tall buildings at a bound). Thus the most significant part of each program only lasts approximately thirty seconds when we are privileged to see the operation in which Steve Austin is transformed into the Six Million Dollar Man. He has escaped from death and so, we hope, will we.

Though we may not think of it as such, he is a "good" Frankenstein figure, a mediating creation who contains within himself two opposing worlds—the world of the natural body and the world of the machine. Steve Austin represents "life kept from death," and Frankenstein represents "death brought to life"; the differences are not extensive.

The Six Million Dollar Man also represents the resolution of a problem that has long plagued man: how do we come to terms with technology? Humanists fear technology as intrinsically dehumanizing and depersonalizing, while scientists are fascinated by its power and possibilities.

When Steve Austin becomes a Six Million Dollar Man, we finally know how the "battle" between the forces of nature and those of technology will be resolved. We will become part machine and the dialectic will be reconciled.

Our fascination with machines has led to a horrendous incorporation of ourselves *into* them in our collective daydreams. And what will the world be like when Six Million Dollar Men and Bionic Women have given place to Twelve or even Twenty-Four Million Dollar Men and Women? At what point does the man-machine collapse into the machine with mobility and intelligence?

For the moment all is well—and Steve Austin is, fortunately, a humane and intelligent figure. But what will we do if, at some future date, he goes berserk (as the audio-animatronic version of President Lincoln did at Disneyland until it was "controlled")? And what will happen if, when we are all Six Million Dollar Men and Women, someone learns how to "control" us?

The Six Million Dollar Man is not to be taken lightly. Our intoxication with him and his exploits has roots far deeper than we suppose. The relation between man and machines has become today's critical issue; we all have been taught that "if you can't lick them, join them." But what will the cost be? Much more, I fear, than six million dollars.

Part 4

Advertising

Analyzing the Advertisement

A METHODOLOGY FOR ANALYZING ADVERTISING

I would like to say somthing about the methods and techniques which may be used in analyzing advertising. Although it may seem strange to spend time dealing with "interruptions" in programs or magazine articles (or "good news" as McLuhan describes advertising), the fact is that advertising is a thirty *billion* dollar a year industry and it has considerable effect on our media, society, and psyches.

In our system of financing televison, for example, programs exist basically as carriers of advertising messages, so in studying advertising I am focusing on a critical aspect of our mass communications system, the aspect which makes everything else possible. This is not to suggest that magazines, newspapers, and television programs are not culturally significant, both as carriers or examples of popular art forms (whose limitations and appeals are worth considering) and as "documents" reflecting socially significant matters. It is to argue that advertisements are also important, and whatever can be said about the way programs function (as far as being socializing agents and providers of role models) can also be said about advertisements.

The considerations that follow apply to all kinds of advertising, though, of course, the medium in which the advertisement appears must be taken into consideration. I will focus here on printed advertisements, though the same methodology can be applied, in modified form, to commercials.

ANALYSIS OF ADVERTISEMENTS

1. *Offer a complete and detailed description and analysis of the components in the advertisement.* In the case of magazine and newspaper advertisements, it is generally possible to present the advertisement itself,

but this is not sufficient. Something should be said about each of the following topics.

A. How would we best describe what might be called the general *ambience* of the advertisement. What mood does it strive to create and for what purposes?

B. The design of the advertisement should be described, with emphasis upon whether it uses axial balance (and is "formal") or some other kind of arrangement. The amount of graphic material, as contrasted with the amount of written material, should also be mentioned.

C. Related to the general design of the advertisement is the matter of the use of white space. Is the advertisement "busy" (with a number of elements competing for attention, as in a typical supermarket advertisement) or "simple," with just a few design elements and a great deal of white or blank space (as in many perfume advertisements or other "high class" advertisements).

D. What significant images and symbols are used in the advertisement? What states of consciousness or fantasy do these images and symbols stimulate? (An *image* is a mental picture of something held by people which is indicative of a general orientation they have; a *symbol* is an object that has cultural significance—in that it stands for something else—which has conscious and unconscious meaning to individuals and to groups of people. These definitions are not complete, but they give some kind of an idea of what the terms mean.)

E. What kind of language is used in the advertisement? Is the language meant to provide information or create some kind of an emotional response, or both? What specific techniques are used by the copywriter: humor, rhyme, and meter, and what "definitions" are offered by the advertisement which might conflict with more generally accepted definitions of things? That is, how do advertisements define "happiness," "joy," "sexy," "love," etc.

F. What type faces are used and what effect is created by the use of the particular faces?

G. What is the item being advertised and what is its specific role and function in American society?

H. When figures are involved, we should consider such matters as their facial expressions, poses, body language, dress, hairstyles, ages, implied relationships, and social class, amongst other things.

I. Where is the action in the advertisement taking place and what is the importance of this locale? How does the background give meaning to the figures in the advertisement? (We sometimes talk about "figure-ground" relationships in visual aesthetics to stress the importance of ground supplying meaning to figures. In the same light, we can take the advertisement itself as a "figure" and relate it to American society and culture as the "ground.")

J. What theme or themes are suggested by the advertisement? I make a distinction here between the notion of *theme,* which is what the advertisement is about, and *plot,* which is what is taking place in the advertisement, what the figures in the advertisement are doing. Thus figures may be smoking or drinking soda pop, which would be the plot, but the theme might be passion and sex.

K. The advertisement represents a "moment in time," and this "frozen moment" must be analyzed for its meaning and significance for the people in a given culture. What reference systems do people have which enable them to interpret an advertisement "correctly" (as far as the advertiser is concerned, that is). Are there differences between the codes of the creators and those of the receivers of the messages in advertisements (and other popular art forms)?

It is important that this description be offered, even if, in the case of newspaper or magazine advertisements, the advertisement itself is available. This is because it is necessary to call attention to the various parts of the advertisement, which may escape the notice of the casual viewer of the advertisement or commercial.

The process of focusing attention on the details of an advertisement may also serve the function of forcing the analyst to take matters into consideration that he might have neglected. Also, I might point out, the actual analysis of symbols and images is often, in itself, a complicated matter that calls for an understanding of psychoanalytic concepts, as well as a knowledge of history, sociology, and a number of other things.

For example, when we come to analyzing significant "images," we find all kinds of things to think about. We frequently encounter *distortion* in figures, *grotesques, stereotyped* figures (such as the sexpot in the bikini, the dumb housewife, the schlemiel, the aristocrat, ad infinitum) and *dissociated* or split figures, amongst other things. We then must decide what, within the context of the advertisement and American culture, the image means.

Obviously this kind of interpretative analysis is somewhat speculative and will be attacked by scientific positivists on the one hand, and merchandizers and advertisers on the other. But to coin the language of the game theorists, the analysis of advertisements offers a "high risk, high gain" kind of activity, and until (if ever) an empirical approach is developed, this somewhat impressionistic and image-inative kind of analysis is all that we have to explore *meaning* in ads.

Some important work on the analysis of images has been done by Roland Barthes, a French sociologist and semiologist, and his essay "The Rhetoric of the Image" provides a useful example of how to deal with the complexity of images. Barthes asks:

> How does meaning enter the image? Where does meaning end? and if it ends, what is there beyond? These are the questions one should ask in subjecting the image to a metabolical analysis of the messages which it can contain. We make it considerably easier for ourselves from the beginning if we study only the advertising image. Why? Because in advertising, the signification of the image is certainly intentional: there are certain attributes of the product which make up *a priori* the signifieds of the advertising message, and these signifieds have to be transmitted as clearly as possible.[1]

Advertising, because it has a specific mission, creates images with certain functions. (I might point out, and this is one of my fundamental assumptions, that the images also contain a good deal more than the advertisers intended.)

There are three messages in images for Barthes. He takes an advertisement showing a half-opened mesh shopping bag, several packages of Panzani spaghetti, Parmesan cheese, tomato sauce, tomatoes, onions, peppers, and a few words of text all against a red background. Then he "creams off," as he puts it, the messages contained in this simple image-advertisement. "The image immediately delivers a primary message, of linguistic substance; its supports are the caption, which is marginal, and the labels, which themselves are inserted into the very nature of the scene, as if they had just been tossed there." The essential message, as far as linguistic substance is concerned, is the name of the company doing the advertising. Next he deals with what he calls the "pure image": "This image immediately delivers a series of discontinuous signs. Here at first (the order is immaterial, for these signs are not linear), there is the idea of return from the market; this signified itself implies two positive values: that of the freshness of the products and that of the purely household use to which they are to be put; its signifier is the gaping string bag which lets the provisions spill onto the table as if 'unpacked'." Intimately connected with the above is the whole matter of marketing, as contrasted with having tinned and frozen foods and the whole tech-nology and mechanized civilization implied by such items.

Another sign connected with this pure image is: "The connection be-tween the tomato, the pepper and the three colour tints (yellow, green, red) of the poster; its signified as Italy, or rather Italian-ness." The third sign is the idea "of a whole culinary service, as if on the one hand Panzani supplied everything necessary for a compound dish, and if on the other hand the concentrate in the tin was equal to the natural pro-ducts surrounding it, the scene making a bridge as it were between the origin of the products and their final state." And lastly, the composition of the advertisement suggests the idea of a "still-life" painting.

What is important is that Barthes shows a number of ways in which an extremely simple advertisement can be explicated. When we try to analyze advertisements with people and with products that are culturally interesting, the difficulties become much greater. In a sense, we have to ravage history to do justice to any given advertisement. At the turn of the century, there was a school of philosophy, *absolute idealism,* which postulated that everything was connected to everything else and that a change in any one thing meant a change in everything else. Absolute idealists believed in "degrees of truth"—that truth wasn't merely a cor-respondence between a statement and reality (however we got to know it) but rather a quality of being able to explain the relation between things. In a sense, that is what we must do in this kind of analysis.

What makes investigating and considering the cultural consequences of advertising so formidable an intellectual task is that we have to do a number of things at the same time. Not only must we concern ourselves with the components of the advertisement and their symbolic signifi-cance (when appropriate), but we must also keep in the mind the social functions of such advertisements and their social significance.

2. *Identify, as best you can, the specific social functions of the advertise-ment under consideration.* Under this category we consider such matters as:

A. The arousal of anxiety as a means toward selling the product and relieving the anxiety.

B. The socializing function of the advertisement, which provides models to imitate, roles to accept. In this respect, advertising often creates certain kinds of behavior and reinforces other kinds of behavior, all of which are intimately connected to advertising's basic mission—merchandizing.

C. The diversion of attention, through selective attention (and neglect of many areas of society), from social problems and man's social dimensions, and the focusing of attention on personal and private concerns.

D. The creation of a "mass society," full of people who have few shared relations with one another, but who are similar in that they share the same mass communications experience, especially as it applies to knowledge of products and the whole sphere of consumption.

Although there are only a relatively limited number of social functions of advertising, each one of the topics mentioned has enormous significance and is really a universe unto itself. For what we are talking about, really, is *shaping behavior,* and shaping behavior, whether only vaguely realized and even if only for seemingly trivial matters, has important implications for man and society.

This matter is extremely complicated, for there is no doubt a certain kind of reverse feedback at work in the creation of advertisements —namely what might be called the "audience image" which is held in the mind of the creator of the advertisement. The creative director, or whomever is responsible for the advertisement *in the final analysis,* must have a picture of his potential audience (just as every creator has some kind of an idea of the public he is creating for).

It might be argued then, and many advertisers and media people do make this argument, *"well then—we're only giving people what they want!"* This is not exactly the case, however, for what the people want has already been, to a large extent, shaped by the media in its function as a socializing agent. People often want what they've been taught to want and that which they consider within the realm of possibility. But their wants and the parameters within which they think have already been set by the media, as well as other socializing agencies, such as the family and the school. And the family and the school are also affected by the media, in general, and advertising, in particular. No doubt the family is the primary socializing institution in America and in most cultures. But a socializing agency can only socialize people to conform with its basic values, which leaves us with the problem of the socialization of the members of the family, and in particular the mothers, who do most of the work of bringing up the children. What I am suggesting is that the mothers are often unconscious agents, who inculcate in their children the values they have picked up as they grew up.

Is it unreasonable to suggest, then, that a large percentage of these women (and their husbands, too, and teachers) have been affected by the advertisements they see? Thus children are socialized, and given certain ideas, expectations, and values, directly through the advertisements they see and hear, and indirectly through the advertisements their parents have seen and heard.

We know that many young people have become extremely cynical about advertisements. Is it not possible that some of this cynicism has been transferred from advertisements and products to other aspects of society such as government, the family, and our educational institutions? It would be unreasonable to pin all the blame on advertising, but it would be naive, I think, not to recognize that the advertising industry is implicated in the general malaise in this society.

Having described and analyzed the components of the advertisement and considered the social function of the advertisement, we are now ready to deal with our third major topic, the utilization of the advertisement as a document reflecting, directly or indirectly, social and psychological problems and phenomena.

3. *Analyze the advertisement as a reflection, either directly or indirectly, of social problems and phenomena.* In this respect, we can consider the following topics (and here I will list a number of items to be considered).

Drug Abuse	Prejudice
Sexism	Boredom
Pollution	Medical Care Inadequacies
Criminal Behavior	Apathy
Warfare	Authoritarianism
Political Extremism	Conformism
Alienation	Elitism and Privilege
Technology	Racism
Deviant Behavior	Schizophrenia
Neurotic Anxiety	Unemployment
Stereotyped Thinking	Old Age
Poverty	Urban Blight
Divorce and Family Crises	Generational Conflict
Ethnocentrism	Loneliness
Excessive ambition	Lack of Communication with Others

Many of the advertisements are not about these concepts but reflect them and thus function, inadvertently, as indicators of social and psychological malaise. Thus we have to examine with great care the appeals made in advertisements, the characters used in advertisements (including such things as facial expression, clothing, body language, etc.) and those characters excluded (Negroes). In essence, what we must do is psychoanalyze the advertisement and use it as an archaeologist uses a fragment of a pot to reconstruct the society that created the object/advertisement. We should also use the object being advertised in the same manner.

In doing this, we must be conscious of what is in the advertisement and what is excluded. It may be that there is an unconscious (or purposive) attempt to avoid certain problems facing people and society? Perhaps advertisements all have a basic middle-class bias and project a world of moderate affluence which is, it is implied, universal? Negroes were, for a long time, excluded from advertisements that the general public was exposed to, but now they are quite common. But what kind of Negroes are used? Are the Negroes found in advertisements "typical," or do they, also, conform to general middle-class notions of what Negroes are like or should be like?

The copy in advertisements is particularly useful in analyzing the cultural significance of a given advertisement. Every word should be scrutinized for its connotations and denotations, and we should be particularly careful about discovering stereotypes, formulas (do it this way, or everybody does it this way), devious kinds of arguments, the use of non-sequiturs, etc.[2]

For a brief example of what may be done with the language of advertising, let us look at an analysis made by Jules Henry in *Culture Against Man* of a cosmetics advertisement:

> Consider the advertisement for *Pango Peach,* a new color introduced by Revlon in 1960. A young woman leans against the upper rungs of a ladder leading to a palm thatched bamboo tree house. *Pango Peach* are her *sari,* her blouse, her toe and finger nails, and the cape she holds. A sky of South Pacific blue is behind her, and the cape, as it flutters in the wind, stains the heavens *Pango Peach.* "From east of the sun—west of the moon where each tomorrow dawns..." beckons the ad, in corny pecuniary lingo. But when you are trying to sell nail polish to a filing clerk with two years of high school you don't quote Dylan Thomas! The idea of the ad is to make a woman think she is reading real poetry when she is not, and at the same time to evoke in her the specific fantasy that will sell the product...
>
> In the ad *Pango Peach* is called "A many splendoured coral... pink with pleasure... a volcano of color!" It goes on to say that "It's a full ripe peach with a world of difference... to be worn in big, jucy slices. Succulent on your lips. Sizzling on your fingertips ... Go Pango Peach... your adventure in paradise." Each word of the advertisement is carefully chosen to tap a particular yearning and hunger in the American woman. "Many splendoured," for example, is a reference to the novel and movie *Love is a Many Splen-*

doured Thing, a tale of passion in an Oriental setting. "Volcano" is meant to arouse the latent wish to be a volcanic lover and to be loved by one. The mouthful or oral stimuli—"ripe," "succulent," "juicy,"—puts sales resistance in double jeopardy because mouths are even more for kissing than eating. "Sizzling can refer only to *l'amour a la folie...*

There is a great deal to be done with analyzing advertising as a social and cultural force and I hope that the techniques described in this essay will provide a methodology for investigating this subject in a more profound and serious manner.

NOTES

1. Roland Barthes, "The Rhetoric of the Image," in *Working Papers in Cultural Studies,* Spring 1971, published by the Centre for Contemporary Cultural Studies, University of Birmingham, England.
2. See S.I. Hayakawa, *Language in Thought and Action,* which has two chapters dealing with the general subject.

Pale Horse, Pale Bather:

An Analysis of the White Horse Advertisement with the Lady in the Bath

This advertisement shows a young lady sitting in a bath, with her left hand on a faucet and her right hand holding a glass of White Horse Blended Scotch Whiskey. She stares ahead wistfully, as if in a trance. To the left of the bathtub a white horse stands, partially enveloped in clouds of steam. Above the horse a light fixture with three lamps glows softly. The horse and the light fixture are reflected in a mirror. The girl has strawberry blonde hair which is knotted on top of her head in a large bun. The bath is an old-fashioned one, with ornamental gold legs and gold faucets.

A bottle of White Horse Blended Scotch Whiskey, occupying the visual center of attention on the page, lies directly underneath her right hand, so that our eye moves from the bottle of liquor to the glass of liquor to her right arm and then to her head and then, along her extended left hand, to the mournful white horse. A thick white and gold rug covers the floor of the room and a few lillies can be seen at the extreme right of the page.

The advertisement has little textual material. At the top left in white and hardly noticeable (perhaps eight-point type) we find "blended scotch whiskey, 86 proof, Four Roses distillers Co., N.Y.C. Sole Importers for the U.S.A." The basic message which is centered at the bottom of the pages reads, "You can take a White Horse anywhere." That is all. This is part of a campaign run by White Horse, which uses the same textual material but shows people in varying activities.

I would describe the ambience of the advertisement as romantic and fantastic; it seems to be a daydream and has a surrealistic quality, with a white horse standing in a bathroom partially lost in billows of steam. Though the advertisement is rather simple, as far as the copy is concerned, it actually presents us with a rather complex and difficult (to explicate) collection of visual symbols. It is hard to fathom this advertisement because the creator probably concerned himself with creating an advertisement that would attract attention through its use of fantasy and incongruity. But while the creator of this advertisement may not have had much *in mind,* what we find is quite interesting, and it might be suggested that this advertisement tells us much more about American life than it thinks it does.

As Leo Bogart has pointed out in *Strategy in Advertising,* "Headlines, slogans, text and logotypes convey symbolic meanings. So do the illustrations of products, people, and backgrounds which evoke whatever associations the advertiser has in mind—and often many that he hasn't" (p. 125). It is possible, then, to explore this advertisement on several levels.

The first level would be that of its mission as far as the advertiser is concerned. In this respect we have the matter of attracting the attention of the magazine reader by presenting him with a bizarre picture—a woman in a bath and her white horse standing by. A woman in a bath is an arresting image, especially if there is a promise of seeing her body. All we see of her, however, is her head, two arms, and right foot, whose toes are seen emerging from the billowing suds which fill the bath.

The advertisement suggests fantasy and romance, which, by inference, we can refer to the liquor she is drinking. Drink enough White Horse and you too will be seeing imaginary (if that's what they are) animals. You too will be able to *escape* from reality. The copy is not particularly interesting. The word "take" suggests power and capacity and the word "anywhere" has something to do with freedom, travel, not being bound by conventions. This message is supported by the unconventional image above it.

The second level involves the *unintended* associations and messages which can be discerned in the advertisement. This kind of analysis involves explicating the significance of symbols and artifacts in terms of the way they reflect cultural attitudes and ideas.

For example, we ought to ask ourselves what symbolic significance the white horse has in this advertisement? The horse is a complex symbol, and the white horse is an even more difficult one. The horse is a symbol of freedom and also of potency—the stallion. This sexual aspect of the horse has been discussed by Germaine Greer in *The Female Eunuch:*

> What the young (girl) rider feels is not that the horse is a projection of her own physical ego, but that it is an *other* which is responding to her control. What she feels is a potent love calling forth a response. The control required by riding is so strong and subtle that

it hardly melts into the kind of diffuse eroticism that theorists. . . would have us believe in. For many girls who are beginning to get the picture about the female role, horse-riding is the only opportunity they will ever have to use their strong thighs to embrace, to excite and to control. George Eliot knew what she was doing when she described Dorothea Brooke's passion for wild gallops over the moors in *Middlemarch*. It is part and parcel of her desire to perform some great heroism, to be free and noble (pp. 73, 74).

The white horse, particularly in American culture, brings to mind heroes such as the Lone Ranger and *his* white horse, Silver. We also think of knights and Prince Charmings on white horses. In such cases the white horse combines the notions of chivalry, innocence, and heroism.

But where is the Prince Charming who should be on the White Stallion? The woman, whose profile is presented to us (she takes no notice of us) is beautiful, but is she loved? This may not be important because she has her beloved bottle of Scotch, which she has taken into her bathroom with her. Alcohol is a depressant and, in the long run, severely limits the sex drive. Is the woman an alcoholic? Must she have a drink even while taking a bath, which itself is symbolic of baptism and redemption. Is she lonely?

The woman is a strawberry blonde. Her hair color combines the innocence of the blonde and the passion of the redhead. In our culture (and in much of the world), there is a general equation of whiteness and lightness with "good" and blackness and darkness with "evil." Women with dark hair are symbolic of seductiveness and mystery and perhaps even danger. But if blondes are childlike and innocent, they are also distant and cold, fitting (in our imagination's eye) the stereotype we have of nordic types.

Curiously enough, the color of the woman's hair and the Scotch are similar—both a light amber. Most Americans prefer "light" Scotch, though the color of liquor is controlled by artificial dyes and chemicals. In fact, the average American, though he thinks he prefers "light" Scotch, cannot describe what he means by "light" and, further, cannot (if his nose in pinched and he cannot smell) tell the difference between Scotch and other kinds of liquor.

The very fact that the woman has her bottle of Scotch with her is significant. The Scotch is an expression of emancipation—she is not drinking some sweet woman's drink, and she's got the bottle in case she wants more. Curiously enough, many of the women's drinks (or drinks that were known as feminine) are now popular with men. And women play a major role in the purchase of liquors. As Charles Winick says in *The New People:* "At the present time, a woman makes every third liquor purchase and every tenth married woman actually buys her own favorite brands and ignores her husband's wishes. As new brands have been created for women, 'soft' and 'delicate' taste is an increasing theme of liquor advertising'' (p. 148). Thus, directing an advertisement for Scotch at women through the use of images significant to women is not as farfetched a scheme as it might seem to be.

One of the basic appeals in this advertisement is to what might be called "good living." This can be seen in the luxurious nature of the appointments—the gilded legs of the bathtub, the deep texture of the rug and towel, and the fresh flowers in the bathroom. But all of this serves to mask the real reason people have for drinking—namely getting drunk, either because they are lonely or cannot cope with their problems, or some similar difficulty.

Ernest Dichter, the eminent motivation researcher, has done some research for the liquor industry:

> ... we found that the real reason for the large number of brands in existence is not the fact that they are truly different. Probably the only real reason most people have for drinking, apart from the semi-rationalization of being social or relaxed, is to put it bluntly, to get drunk. It would be a shameful thing, however, for a person to go into a store or into a bar and ask for a drink simply to get drunk. Instead of that, we have developed an elaborate ritual. We want a martini, with just the right amount of vermouth and one or two twists of lemon peal; we are very intent upon buying a specific brand of liquor and not accepting a substitute for it. Our own tests indicate that the majority of people cannot distinguish between one brand of liquor and another. . . . The reason for this insistence on a special brand is partly to cover up the true reason of promiscuity in drinking and to substitute for it the illusion of individuality.

Thus, in the context of the advertisement being discussed, White Horse Brand Scotch suggests individuality and distinctive taste (the brand) and success (the kind of liquor). Scotch is basically a middle-class and upper-class drink, and middle-class and upper-class people attain a spurious kind of individuality through their demonstration of preference for specific brands of Scotch.

In this advertisement, the rather elegant hairdo of the woman and the surroundings all reinforce this class element. What disturbs things is the essential vulgarity of a woman, or anyone, drinking in the bathtub. There is a tension established by offering conflicting symbols: the bottle of liquor and the glass (guilt, evil), and the bath (innocence, baptism).

This advertisement was not easy to analyze and does not yield any startling insights, but I selected it because it has very little copy and thus forced me to deal with images and symbols. It also involves a major problem facing American society—that of the abuse of alcohol (in particular) and drugs (in general). But even though this advertisement has little copy to discuss and has a few items—the lady, the bottle of scotch, the rug, the white horse, etc., it still does tell us something of interest. And what it tells us, or to be more specific, what we can discern from it is profoundly disquieting.

What is most disturbing is the need for alcohol even in the most incongruous situations, and the matter-of-factness about the lady as she sips her Scotch. She symbolizes a spurious kind of emancipation which is fostered in women in our society, the "you've come a long way, baby" theme which equates freedom with the unrestricted opportunity to drink or smoke. But underneath, mirrored in the rather sad and perhaps even bitter face of the lady in the bathtub is a spark of recognition. She seems to lack affectivity, and in that rather painful and frozen stare there is a message for all of us.

It might be asserted, then, that although this advertisement is one which consciously, or on the conscious level, tries to sell liquor, on the unconscious level it works in the other direction. It is doubtful whether the creator of this advertisement or the casual reader would sense this, or make the connection (consciously, that is) between the expression on the lady's face, women's role, the liberation movement, and alcoholism. But I believe all these elements are there, and because they are there, this advertisement is quite valuable to the student of American society.

Advertisements such as this one are like Freudian slips, which reveal a great more than they seem. To read them correctly we must be aware of what Erich Fromm calls "The Hidden Language," the language of signs and symbols and significations. When we learn this language, the lady in the bath, though she is mute, has a great deal to tell us.

Women and Advertising:

Selling with Sex

I

It all began in the Garden of Eden! God had told Adam and *his* woman (as yet unnamed) not to taste the Tree of Life, but the wily serpent talked her into it.

> And the serpent said unto the woman,
> "Ye shall not surely die: for God doth know that in
> the day ye eat thereof, then your eyes shall be opened
> and ye shall be as gods, knowing good and evil."

> And when the woman saw that the tree was good for
> food, and that it was pleasant to the eyes, and a
> tree to be desired to make one wise, she took of the
> fruit thereof, and did eat, and gave also unto her
> husband with her; and he did eat.

As a result of this act, Adam and his wife discovered they were naked, hid themselves from God, and were ultimately thrown out of the Garden.

> And the Lord God said unto the woman,
> "What is it that thou hast done?"
> And the woman said, "The serpent beguiled me,
> and I did eat."

There were further consequences: snakes were made to slither on their bellies, women would henceforth bring forth their children "in sorrow" and be ruled by their husbands, and man was sentenced to hard labor for life. The impact on the consciousness of man of these first few pages of the Bible has been remarkable, if you think about it. For here, in a very condensed form, we find the basic myths which have played a major part in the shaping of our societies (in the western world, at least) and the development of many of our institutions and attitudes.

The women's liberation movement is, in large measure, an attempt to overthrow God's punishment for having "tempted" man. The real villain was the snake, the most subtle creature of the field, and the prototype of the advertising man. The snake *beguiled* the first women, and advertising men have been beguiling women ever since. Accordingly, it is fitting that we examine the relationship between women and sex and advertising, keeping in mind the mythico-historical relationship found in the Bible.

II

What has happened is that as liberal secular thought has developed, the "sacredness" of woman's role as a housewife and the concomitant notion that she was somehow a subservient being suddenly lost credence, forcing women to confront the reality of their situation. Until the housewife's role lost its sacred character, being a housewife provided a certain psychic sustenance, as sacred vocations generally do. Women had been convinced that raising children earned them the love of God; in addition, as is often the case when we deal with the sacred, there seemed no other possibilities. Thus, in a sense, women were making the best of what they now consider a "raw" deal—they had a justification for a job that they had to do anyway, or believed they had to do.

It might be pointed out that the same loss of sacrality and sacramentality has taken place in agriculture, which, stripped of its divine nature, reveals itself as a time-consuming and nasty job. Less than ten percent of the population sees fit to engage in it now, and a high proportion of those who do so are poor, ill-treated migrant workers who pick various crops and have no alternatives.

When the sacred quality of the housewife's task is doubted, and ultimately cast off, then other relationships are looked upon rationally and logically, not as "ordained" somehow by divine command. In such cases, the institutions of society and the attitudes of large numbers of males, *and through complicity, females,* are revealed as sexist. Although there are many sexist institutions in society, from the family itself to our modern universities, I believe that it is advertising, more than any other one, that has indoctrinated and reinforced sexist ideas.

What we find is a spurious kind of worship of the goddess of beauty, so that women will not remember that, for the most part, they are treated like drudges. It is a classic case of mystification; we idealize *woman* as the incarnation of divine beauty, love, and goodness, but we treat our *women* in scornful and dehumanizing ways. This process has been beautifully described by Germain Greer in *The Female Eunuch:*

> Because she is the emblem of spending ability and the chief spender, she is also the most effective seller of this world's goods. Every survey has shown that the image of an attractive woman is the most effective advertising gimmick. She may sit astride the mudguard of a new car, or step into it ablaze with jewels; she may lie at a man's feet stroking his new socks; she may hold the petrol pump in a challenging pose, or dance through the woodland glades in slow motion in all the glory of a new shampoo; whatever she does her image sells. The gynolatry of our civilization is written large upon its face, upon hoardings, cinema screens, television, newspapers, magazines, tins, packets, cartons, bottles, all consecrated to the reigning deity, the female fetish (pp. 51, 52).

Greer sees this idol as an unreal doll—a "perfect" creation whose perfection signifies that she is not human but rather an idealization, an abstraction, a fantasy.

In this respect, this "idea of women" is treated very much like certain human divinities and kings, in that every action is circumscribed and the price of divinity is paralysis and, at times, death. "How," asks the sexist, "can you say this is a sexist society when we put woman up on a pedestal and worship her?" The answer is, of course, that while *woman* may be on a pedestal, *women* are not.

Not all women have seen through the mythification and idealization of woman; some because they lack the intelligence and others because they lack the courage. But this is not of any great importance, for once the bubble bursts, it cannot be recreated. What is important to recognize is that there is a sociological dimension to myth. It is clear in the Bible but not so clear in the mannequin or in something like the Miss America contest. Harvey Cox, in "Miss America and the Cult of the Girl," explains how the Miss America contest is tied to ancient myths and represents "a re-emergence of cults of the pre-Christian fertility goddesses."

III

Cox argues that the Miss America contest has two functions. The first is to help "initiate," gain personal identity by providing a model to imitate; the second is to help integrate the values of her society—namely "endless upward mobility, competitive consumerism and anxious cynicism." Miss America is for Cox an idol, the Queen of Commodities, whose values lack ultimacy and who cannot bestow *real* identity, since she is only a stereotype—and ultimately a tool.

After all, Miss America's main job, once crowned, is to peddle things. There is an irony to this, for even our queens are manipulated and forced to exploit their "beauty" for generally base purposes. Miss America, herself, is a classic example of the process I have been discussing—the idealization of the female, in the abstract, and her degradation in the concrete. Her life is not her own once she is crowned, and she spends a year of her life as a mink-coated and luxuriously treated lackey of the advertising industry.

Miss America has more significance than meets the proverbial eye, though her basic function is to be an "eye-pleaser," because myth has an ideological content that is not apparent. This was pointed out by Roland Barthes in his remarkable book, *Mythologies*. What myth does, suggests Barthes, is to take practices and institutions which are *historical* (created by man, hence capable of being changed) and suggest, through mythification, that these practices and institutions are *natural* (hence eternal and not capable of being changed). In essence, myths are ahistorical and support the status quo by arguing that whatever *is,* as Pope puts it, is right!

Thus there is a bourgeois content to myth; it is apparent in the Miss America myth, since she is nothing more than a virginal huckster. She can be looked at but not touched; the desires she engenders in those who gaze upon her are to be translated into sales, it is hoped. She also symbolizes the good-looking girl who can rise in the world due to her beauty, but this, in turn, only reinforces her degradation, for she becomes a "sex object," as the women liberation advocates put it, and is herself "consumed" as a kind of living showpiece. In this role she is a living ornament, the most remarkable exemplification of conspicuous consumption—whose basic function is to bolster the ego of the male who has "bought her" for ego gratification and sex.

An article in the July 31, 1972 *San Francisco Chronicle* by Judith Anderson is very much to the point here. The headline reads "Beauty Contest Made Her a 'Misfit'," and deals with Sharon Brown, Miss USA, 1961. It starts with a quote from her, "I'm sorry I won. I wouldn't go through that year again for anything," though she also mentioned that her title "opened doors," and taught her how to "handle" people.

Even now, ten years after she won her title, she finds it rather difficult to relate to men in an ordinary manner, for "equipped with her vital statistics they've gleaned from write-ups in trade publications, male customers stand across the showroom and stare." The statistics are symbolic of the dehumanization implicit in the beauty contests, for until the rise of women's liberation, beauty queens were inevitably described in terms of their "measurements," with a near approximation of an *hourglass* figure being considered ideal. The men know how big Miss Brown's breasts are, and in possession of these magic numbers, "possess" her in some magic way. The hourglass figure numbers are the *formula* for the ideal female, the symmetrically perfect piece of ass.

This "beauty" creates all kinds of complications. For the beauty queen, who is admired, basically, for her body, the peril of gaining weight and growing old are a constant source of fear and danger. For the men who stare at beauty queens but cannot possess them, there is a sense of frustration. The ordinary women pales by comparison, for the ordinary man has erotic fantasies stimulated by beauty queens and, in particular, by advertisements that hound him continually. As Raphael Patai says in *Myth and Modern Man:*

> It has often been observed that sexual appetite in man is greater than sexual capacity. This means that even when he has as much sex as he can take, he still wants more. . . . Herein lies one of the problems that sex poses to man.
>
> Another is the inability of the male to possess sexually those women who attract him and excite him the most. The average, ordinary man in our modern world can have sexual intercourse with women even without using the services of prostitutes. But the women whom he can enjoy are, of necessity, his own female counterparts; in other words, average, ordinary women. Having such women may satisfy man's sexual hunger, but not his erotic fantasies. In them, the male will continue to imagine himself conquering and possessing the most exquisite women, the aesthetically, sexually, erotically, and emotionally most attractive specimens of the female sex. With women, the same situation obtains in reverse (pp. 285-86).

All of this is part of what Patai calls "the fantasy of the perfect sex partner." This fantasy is literally forced upon man by the continual bombardment (he says we are "literally assaulted") by the image of the sex goddess, beauty queen, model, mannequin, who exploits her sexuality to sell merchandise. She does this by exciting men but giving them no gratification; the only hope they have is that by purchasing certain products, they can, in some mysterious manner, "possess" her.

As Patai puts in:

> The movies, television, magazine and newspaper ads, posters, store-window mannequins, life-size, smaller than life, bigger than life, in colors or in black-and-white, in partial or total undress, in all kinds of alluring and enticing positions with the most express indications of availability, willingness, readiness to welcome you to their arms. . . have the combined and cumulative effect of making many men dissatisfied with whatever sexual activity is available to them (p. 286).

All of this frustration sets the stage for the ordinary man to become a "Sexual Superman." By using various products, he becomes transformed into an irrestible male. This is a basic theme is a large number of commercials, which show that product knowledge is the *real* key to a woman's heart—or at least her body. (The same thing holds for women, who once rid of body odor or pimples, have thrilling romances and magnificent love affairs.)

IV

If you observe television commercials carefully, you will notice that, generally speaking, there is no middle ground between the sex goddess and the dreary housewife. There seem to be two basic roles for women—and I admit that I am oversimplifying here, to make a point—brides and housefraus.

Bride-Beauty	Housefrau—Old Bag
Lover	Mother
Sex, The Bedroom	Clothes, The Laundry

These two archetypes are involved with two spheres of activity. For the young girl, there is the world of love, romance, sex, and the great climactic event, the marriage. The order of these activities is quite mixed; it used to be love, bride, and fornication, but the development of the pill has changed all that. The children who sing "first comes love, then comes marriage, then comes Junior in the baby carriage," don't know what they are talking (i.e. singing) about.

What is curious is that it doesn't take very long for the Bride-Beauty to become the Housefrau-Old Bag in the popular imagination; this is a basic cliché of advertising and popular culture in America. The process is speeded up because wives are real human beings, who get tired and grow older, who aren't always perfectly dressed and are not perfect illusions. In contrast, the media, and commercials in particular, are full of expertly made up, beautifully dressed, and physically attractive illusions, with whom it is impossible to compete.

It may very well be, then, that all those "dumb" housewives who get so excited about getting spots out of Junior's dungarees deserve a bit of sympathy. They have been desexualized, and their desperation manifests itself in the desire to be, at least, a good housefrau and thus be worthy of love and admiration in *that* role, since their status as a sex object has been taken away from them. Beautiful women don't have to get the wash clean; ordinary women had better! In effect, they have "renounced sex" (even if only to the point of acquiescing in being made into old bags) and accepted the good housekeeper role, in which "cleanliness is next to godliness." So washing clothes (and such) is an unconscious attempt to rid oneself of the stigma of having been responsible for Adam's eating the apple; the housewife gets rid of dirt and sinfulness, and her clean clothes earn man's and God's love.

One of the great ironies that is involved in this matter of advertising and feminine roles is that the desperate and frenzied race to marriage and motherhood, and ultimately the housefrau role, is destructive of sexuality, so that sexuality and glamour lead, ultimately, to their own destruction. Studies of teenage consumer behavior show that purchasing things gives identity and status. And according to a study made by *Seventeen,* the average teenage girl spends a great deal of money and time shopping for clothes and cosmetics, as well as records, cameras, soft drinks, radios, etc.

Seventeen's study showed that the typical teenage girl shops for clothes and cosmetics six days a week, and when they purchase things, they are concerned about style and not cost. Since there is a 25-billion-dollar youth market now, it is reasonable to assume that teenage girls spend some $12 billion a year on shopping for various items. They do this because they have been taught to do this by the advertising industry, which creates fears of inadequacy and loneliness in those who aren't stylish and attractive, and by the behavior of their parents, who have been socialized into consumermania by the advertising industry and American culture itself.

What is remarkable is that these girls don't pay any attention to the "fate worse than death" (in the advertising world view) that awaits them after marriage and motherhood, in particular. They become so obsessed about being loved and getting married that they fail to see the dreary end of it all—the dipsy housefrau excited about how clean she gets the clothes. Their mad rush into marriage blinds them to the fact that, as advertisements show, women want to be loved so they can, eventually, be hated. The descent from the bedroom to the laundry room is rapid.

V

This phenomenon is exacerbated by what is called "The Stud Husband Phenomenon," which describes men with the *cowboy* syndrome. Men with this affliction cannot be emotionally intimate but, instead model their behavior on the strong, cold silent he-man seen in movies and advertisements. According to Dr. Alfred Auerback of the University of

California School of Medicine, these *cowboys* learn to be studs from "watching James Bond movies, from media advertising and from the Playboy philosophy...." Their basic orientation is a predatory one, and their dealings with women are based upon the goal of nonrelational sexual exploitation, with little concern for human feelings.

Thus the cowboy (the *boy* in the term should be noted) who supposedly loves his horse and the schoolmarm, in that precise order, is essentially an infantile personality who cannot relate to women, as persons, though he probably idealizes them in the abstract.

He is in love with the *idea* of the schoolmarm—the lovely woman who brings culture to the wilderness—and not with the schoolmarm herself. This is one reason why he is able to renounce love with such equanimity. The modern urban cowboy male is nothing but a predator out to exploit women, and it is most unlikely that he can ever move beyond this kind of relationship, even though he probably also idealizes the eternal female.

VI

This idealization of the female has taken a number of bizarre forms. The most remarkable—for it allies our Puritanism with our contempt for women—involves the practice (no longer in vogue) of eliminating navels in photographs of women, or covering them up on television programs, such as *I Dream of Jeanie.* Until fairly recently, *Seventeen* airbrushed out all navels—under the assumption, I imagine, that a sixteen-year-old girl looking at a bare navel would be driven wild with sexual frenzy. But such reverse-fetishism is absurd, since the very purpose of *Seventeen* is to turn pubescent thirteen-year-old adolescents into irresistible sex goddesses. Why should navels be so stimulating?

The answer probably has something to do with the fact that the navel is symbolic of our fallen state, of the fact that we are all born of woman. Many children, as a matter of fact, think that babies are born through navels until they learn better. Adam had no navel. You can tell by examining his picture in the Sistine Chapel—unless, that is, the editors of *Seventeen* got there early.

It may very well be that the covered navel represents the maginot line of American Puritanism, an anachronistic residue of an asceticism that has long since been rejected by American culture. The American navel was overwhelmed by the European bikini, and with the loss of the navel, Puritanism has given up the ghost. The absurd contradiction in magazines and other mass media between erotic advertisements and covered navels has been resolved, with one more victory for sensate culture—but not a victory for women.

For after the navel fell, there came the bare tit or "nipple school" of advertising, which is very popular abroad and is beginning to be accepted here. Puritanism may be dead, but it is hard to get it to give up the ghost, and cultural lag will ensure that it will hold sway for a while longer yet, though it is no longer a vital force with most Americans. What bare tit advertising does is to carry further the idealization of the female by turning the clock back to the Garden, once again, and portraying woman as Eve. In Paradise, as we learn in *Genesis:* ". . . they were both naked, the man and his wife, and they were not ashamed."

In fact, what we find in *Genesis* is an example of the two roles I discussed earlier. Eve is the prototype of the woman who starts off as Bride-Beauty and quickly becomes Housefrau-Old Bag: "And Adam called his wife's name Eve; because she was the mother of all living. Unto Adam also and to his wife did the Lord God make coats of skins, and clothed them." Both motherhood and the laundry are mentioned right here, and Adam who "gave names to the cattle," also named his wife.

The advertising industry, which is very alert to social movements and new kinds of collective behavior, has latched on to "woman's lib" just as it has co-opted ecology; by nature advertising is parasitic, and it does whatever it can to insure its survival. The *Virginia Slims* campaign tells women "You've come a long way baby," but this is a lie! The campaign slogan, which used the term "baby" is, itself, inept—though the commercials are beautifully done from a technical standpoint. The term *baby* is anathema to liberated women, who rightfully resent being called a "baby" or a "cookie," or anything like that.

But in fact, as our brief survey shows, women are really right back where they started—metaphorically speaking, that is. As a final note, I should say that I believe that women themselves have "cooperated" in their degradation and humiliation, and are not just helpless victims of a dehumanizing and exploitative society. To the extent that they allow themselves to be bamboozled by advertising and consumermania, they help forge the chains that bind them.

The Wednesday Specials as Theatre of the Absurd: The Stuffed Cart (Not the Sad Heart) at the Supermarket

I

The middle-of-the-week supermarket advertisements found in the newspapers are one of the most common and all pervasive kinds of advertisements. They are studies in *banality*—in essense they are lists of items that are available, with certain products given special notoriety because they are reduced-in-price "specials" (used to lure people into stores) or are in season. Some layouts are more orderly than others; some stress different "advantages" one gets in shopping at a particular place, but as a literary genre they do not seem particularly exciting.

Except, of course, that they play a major role in determining how the typical family of four (two adults, two children) will spend about forty dollars that week in the supermarket, and to a certain extent what this family and its pets will eat. On the average, we spend some $2,000-plus a year on food, and most of this is spent at supermarkets, which are probably the most important merchandising institutions in contemporary American society.

These supermarket advertisements are primarily directed to women, who do most of the shopping in supermarkets, yet the advertisements conflict in certain ways with a basic stereotype Americans have of women as essentially emotionally and not particularly orderly and rational. Yet the advertisements themselves are studies in organization and classification, whose basic service is apparently to give information. It may very well be that these advertisements are better described as being pseudo-rational, for though they have a semblance of order and reason, it is well known that once a woman or man is lured into the supermarket, all kinds of impulses leading to irrational purchasing come into play, but such things are not intrinsic to the advertisements themselves.

145

There is actually a whole "psychology" behind these full-page advertisements, which is explained in *Consumer Dynamics in The Super market: A Study of Food Retailing and the Super market Customer:*

> It is rather remarkable considering the important function of super market advertising that so much of it has failed to take into account an understanding feminine trait that bears directly on the form of the ad message itself. The late distinguished author, Shirley Jackson, put it quite bluntly when she described women as thinking characteristically in lists. This mode of thinking, moreover, tends to be particularly present in the practice of the housewifely role. This, in conjunction with those other essential traits that define this same role, such as the compulsion for order and cleanliness, unmistakably adds up to the comments about the shortcomings in current advertising practices [which were based on interviews with women shoppers] (p. 133).

The female, once she becomes a housewife, switches identities and roles, and instead of being a glamorous figure who offers excitement and romance, she becomes a minor administrator. And the lists we see in the supermarket advertisements appeal to this essential "trait," because they appeal to the other side of women (at least as the popular mind sees her) —the housefrau-drudge. The bachelor has made laundry lists; he disposes of this nuisance and relieves himself of the need to make shopping lists (if he did before marriage) when he weds. Thereafter it is the woman, with her "trait" for lists, who takes over these responsibilities, freeing man to be scatterbrained, witless, and useless in the household.

Of course this trait is not present in the single female, except perhaps in latent form. It is when she marries, and in particular when she has children, that time becomes problematical and the housewife must get herself organized and become, if she is small and slender, a petite-bourgeois bureaucrat. Thus men read comics and sports, and dream great dreams of adventure and romance, and women study supermarket advertisements, and heroically fight the battle of the household budget.

The basic function of supermarket advertisements is to serve as a listing of products so that *other advertisements, seen on television and elsewhere can be recalled,* and once brought to mind, convince her to purchase this or that item. There is a tie-in between the amount of money spent on advertising and amount of shelf-space a given product gets, so that the advertising of specific products is related to the mention of specific items in supermarket ads, at least indirectly.

The supermarket advertisement is, then, a remembrance of advertisements past and things past, and to the extent that advertising plays upon fantasies and emotions, the supermarket advertisement is a plot outline which sets in motion a whole world of fantasy and make-believe. *The supermarket advertisement is the American contribution to the Theatre of the Absurd!* Instead of Ionesco playing with phrases from a guide to English for travelers, fifty million American housewifes cook up, so to speak, their own fantasies from the basic plot outline provided on Wednesdays.

It is a pastiche of all the advertisements and all the minidramas and fantasies racing around in the housewife's mind. All the associations and remembrances that are linked to food start working away in her collective unconscious, and she can recall "happy times" in the past, project happiness in the future, and imagine herself in a number of different roles. "Less is more," say the aestheticians, and the less there is in a supermarket advertisement (by way of specific inducements to "ordained" fantasies), the more chance there is for specific and personal dreams and imaginings as they relate to advertisements—and in particular commercials—that have been previously viewed.

Thus the weekly supermarket advertisements serve as "plot outlines" to the great commercials of the past. These commercials, in turn, are mediated or ordained fantasies which set off private ones—and the austerity and minimalness of the supermarket advertisements lead to flamboyant and remarkable personal fantasies in women. It is these fantasies which prevent women from being completely rational in their purchases, though they may believe they are rational and logical.

The image of order and neatness created in the advertisement also is a reflection of the store itself, so we have an art form that, for once, is a perfect representation of "true life." Different supermarket chains project different identities in their advertisements, depending upon what that identity is. And the stores themselves are magnificent examples of industrial "rationalization" in which everything conceivable has been taken into consideration so as to create fantasy and emotions to stimulate sales. The order in the supermarket, like the order in the advertisement, is somewhat fraudulent, for it is not reason but imagination that is served. This is because when we are surrounded by such a fantastic variety of items, our sensorium is disturbed—attacked, so to speak, by the infinity of choice that bewilders us and forces us to seek refuge of some kind. We are strangers in paradise and, like strangers anywhere, we seek something to "hold onto," something familiar which gives us security. Into the void steps the advertised product, offering reassurance and flattering our vanity for just a few pennies more.

There is even a mythological dimension to shopping in a supermarket, for when we become ensconced in the various lanes, we recreate, so to speak, the legend of Theseus and the Minotaur. The supermarket is the *labyrinth* which the housewife must enter every week, an ordeal that is at once boring, stimulating, and costly—for at the end waits the most terrible of monsters, the mixed-up check-out clerk and his malevolent servant, the erratic adding machine.

It is not so farfetched to discuss the supermarket as a labyrinth, for supermarkets do have this quality—especially now that they are getting larger and larger and carrying more products. In the supermarket industry, layout is a perennial problem, and the middle of the store is often called "the jungle." This is because shoppers feel "safer" in the perimeters of the store, where the most important selling features of the supermarket are located—produce, dairy, bakery products, meat, etc. Luring customers from the perimeter to the inner areas of the labyrinth is a major concern, since research indicates that there is a relationship that exists between passing and buying products.

There is also a relationship between the rehearsal of the play (that is, looking at the supermarket advertisements) and the play itself (going shopping). Shopping in a supermarket is, then, a multifaceted experience. It is the enactment of a myriad of private fantasies in the mind of the shopper, it is a performance of a specific and personal kind of "theatre of the absurd," and it is a ritualistic ordeal in a labyrinth which must be "solved" if one is to survive and one's family is to eat that week.

In addition to all the other things I mentioned earlier, the supermarket is the sanctuary of the American shopper—it is the American consumer's cathedral. She goes there once a week just as she goes to church once a week. She gets sustenance—physical and spiritual—from her "experience" there, as well as from her church. She is given a sense of the immense diversity in the world, of man's infinite variety, of all the things that will, she hopes, make her sojourn on earth a better one. It is a hedonistic church, but a church never the less.

As she pushes the cart down the aisles and compulsively and impulsively crams different things into it—cereals and soda pop, bread and wine, beefsteaks and instant cakes, she is taking part in a ritual of deep significance. And the supermarkets have learned something from the churches—both wax fat thanks to one form or another of bingo. The Safeway chain's *Bonus Bingo* campaign raised sales by 13 percent and profits by 39 percent in some areas while it was run.

The Supermarket has flourished because it reflects the American psyche and world view, and because, in the great American evangelical tradition, it reaches out to the American and enables him to show *his sense of the divine* in the mundane, and lose himself in the equivalent of religious ecstasy.

Part 5

Humor

Humor as a System of Communication

One of the things we tend to overlook when we start thinking about humor is that it is *communicated* to us, one way or another. I recently spent an evening at a bar in San Francisco which offers an "open mike" to comedians—professionals and amateurs, and as I watched some of the would-be stand-up comics in front of the mike, I could not help but be impressed by the problems they faced in trying to reach the audience. Some fumbled about, hesitantly; others pulled slips from their pockets with topics for their "routines" listed on them; while others were perfectly at ease and had no trouble relating to everyone.

If you think of it, all humor is presented, one way or another, via the different media available. Stand-up comedians use their voices and gestures and facial expressions (performance is a critical aspect of orally-delivered humor), cartoonists use figures and language, films use characters and dialogues, while writers are limited to the printed word.

Since humor is communication, it can be analyzed using a form of communication "model" that is used for all kinds of communication. This "model" is given on page 153.

Table 5.1: The Communication Model Explicated (Categories and Techniques of Humor)

Categories:	Language	Logic	Identity	Action
Techniques	Allusion	Absurdity	Before/After	Chase Scenes
	Bombast	Accident	Burlesque	Slapstick
	Definition	Analogy	Caricature	Speed
	Exaggeration	Catalogue	Embarassment	Time
	Facetiousness	Coincidence	Eccentricity	
	Irony	Disappointment	Exposure	
	Misunderstanding	Ignorance	Grotesque	
	Over-Literalness	Mistakes	Imitation	
	Puns	Repetition	Impersonation	
	Repartee	Reversal	Infantilism	
	Ridicule	Rigidity	Mimicry	
	Sarcasm	Theme &	Parody	
	Satire	Variation	Scale	
			Stereotype	
			Unmasking	

Depending upon our interests, we can focus upon one or another (or several) of the above different parts of the humor-communication system.

Using the techniques listed in the chart and applying them to any of the forms of humor, it's possible to gain an understanding of *what* it is in the "information" transmitted by the humorist that leads to humor or humorous responses. Of course any one of the items listed in the communication model can be studied. If you focus upon the sender, you do (in effect) biographical and historical criticism; if you focus on the receiver(s), you are involved with essentially sociological concerns—and might, for instance, look at social class, educational level, ethnicity, race, and so on to gain some kind of an understanding of the relationship between humor and its audience.

If you direct your attention upon D, the medium of transmission, you are essentially in the realm of mass media research and must consider what effects and limitations a given medium has upon the humor it transmits. You can't do "sight gags" on radio, for example, and each medium presents certain problems for humorists working within that medium. The last item on the chart involves psychology and social-psychology, in that it focuses upon the purposes the humor serves for the audience and perhaps for the comedian (sender). Thus, some jokes tend to integrate the joke-teller with the group in which he is telling the joke (or do the opposite), which may also involve masked aggression and tension relief on the part of the joke-teller, and numerous other functions for all involved.

The most interesting problem, as far as I am concerned, is to use the techniques to understand how the *information* that we find in humor generates laughter, mirth, joy, and so on. Why we laugh is another matter. There are a number of theories explaining this phenomenon; the most well known one stems from the work of Freud and the psychoanalytic school and relates humor to the release of aggression in masked forms. Another important explanation of why we laugh is that of the cognitive school of psychology, which focuses upon play and paradoxes and shifts that take place in meaning. Gregory Bateson and William Fry, Jr., are two exponents of this approach. In addition, there is the "superiority" theory of Hobbes, who said (in *The Leviathan*): "The passion of laughter is nothing else but sudden glory arising from a sudden conception of some eminency in ourselves by comparison with the infirmity of others, or with our own formerly."

This notion, however, may be a special case of a larger explanation, that of incongruity. The difference between humor and other kinds of information is that humor establishes *incongruous* relationships (meaning) with a *sudden-ness* (timing) that leads us to laugh. I will use incongruity

Table 5.2: The Communication Model and Humor

A	Communicates B	to C	via D	using form E	and technique F	with X effect	for Y purposes
Comedian	Information	Audience	TV	jokes	one of 45	humor	one of the boys
Writer		Public	Radio	cartoons	basic techniques	laughter	tension relief
Cartoonist		Gathering	Print	riddles	(found in accompanying chart)	mirth etc.	masked aggression
Clown		Crowd	Film	plays			sexual arousal
		Self?	Speech	stories			
Sender	Content	Receiver	Medium	Art Form	Technique	Effect	Function

here as "not harmonious, not conforming, inconsistent within itself and lacking propriety," which obviously covers a lot of ground. The matter of humor being "inconsistent within itself" is close to the cognitive theory of humor, mentioned above.

I do not know of anyone who has successfully explained *why* we laugh, but it is possible to show, within reliable limits, *what* techniques generate humor in any example of humor. For example, if we take a joke, we can isolate different techniques to be found operating in the joke and generating the laughter.

Let us take the following joke and analyze it:

A southern redneck walked into a bar in New York with an alligator on a leash. "Do you serve Niggers here?" he asked the barkeeper. "This is New York," answered the bartender. "We serve Negroes." "Okay," said the southerner. "Give me a double scotch, and serve my alligator a Negro."

This joke can be analyzed structurally, as a chain of elements linked together, which leads to humor. The term for this kind of analysis is *syntagmatic,* in the jargon of structuralists. The other important technique in structural analysis is called *paradigmatic* analysis, and works by eliciting polar oppositions in a given work, in an attempt to discern hidden meanings. In actuality, a joke must be analyzed both as a series of elements and as a series of oppositions, as will be demonstrated below.

The joke has the following actions-elements in it.

1. The southerner entering the bar with his alligator.
2. The question asked by the southerner.
3. The response by the bartender.
4. The responses by the southerner, the second of which is the PUNCH LINE.

We can diagram this as follows:

Element 1 + Element 2 + Element 3 + Element 4   (Syntagmatic Structure)
                                  (PUNCH LINE)

                    HUMOR ↙   (Paradigmatic Analysis)

Humor, from the syntagmatic perspective, is connected with the resolution of a "dialectic" which is established by the punch line among elements in an episode. The oppositions found in the joke are charted below:

The South	The North
The Southerner	The Northerner
Redneck Racist	Bartender
Alligators	Negroes
Absurdity	Rationality

Essentially two opposing worlds of belief are posited in the joke, which then terminates in the surprise suggestion of the southerner that his alligator be given a human being (Negro) for a snack. The basic techniques at work in this joke are first, *stereotypes,* and second, *misunderstanding,* or the humor of identity and language, respectively. The punch line is based upon a misunderstanding of the southerner's intention by the bartender, who did not realize the southerner was speaking literally. Listeners to the joke are put off by the term Nigger, while, in fact, the critical matter is the verb *serve.*

Humor is an extremely complicated phenomenon which has resisted the efforts of philosophers, writers, psychologists, and just about everyone else for several thousand years. By recognizing that humor is a system of communication and helping to "disentangle" it, I hope we can make some progress in our efforts to understand what it is and how it works.

Huck Finn as an Existential Hero: Making Sense of Absurdity

The relationship between character and humor is well known. In Constance Rourke's work, *American Humor,* we find the following statement in her foreword:

> . . . Humor is one of those conceits which give form and flavor to an entire character. In the nation, as comedy moves from a passing effervescence into the broad stream of a common possession, its bearings become singularly wide. There is scarcely an aspect of the American character to which humor is not related, few which in some sense it has not governed. It has moved into literature, not merely as an occasional touch, but as a force determining large patterns and intentions. It is a lawless element, full of surprises. It sustains its own appeal, yet its vigorous power invited absorption in that character of which it is a part.[1]

One of my basic assumptions is that humor has distinctive national colorations and that if offers a good deal of information about the assumptions, values, and dispositions of cultures. This is why a novel like *Huckleberry Finn* is considered, by the overwhelming majority of literary scholars, as a great *American* novel. It is because of Twain's mastery of the techniques of humor and his brilliant use of the vernacular, and it is significant because of the light it sheds on American culture.

Until the "discovery" of *Huckleberry Finn* a few decades ago by literary critics, it was seen as a children's book about a young boy's adventures on a raft, and not much different—perhaps not as "good"—as Tom Sawyer. With the development of American Studies and of myth criticism, however, *Huckleberry Finn* has emerged to a position of centrality in American literature. A closer look at the book revealed that the various adventures added up to a devastating attack upon the ugliness of slavery and many other nineteenth-century American institutions; the raft and river became symbols of the pastoral ideal which was to give way to the steamboat, railroad and industrialism; and the very language of the book was seen as a major influence upon American literature.

In almost every respect, Twain's achievement is impressive. The book is an astounding comic tour de force, in which Twain uses a large number of humorous techniques brilliantly. I would like to point out some of these techniques, show how Twain "pulled them off," and say something about their significance as far as the American ethos is concerned.

The book itself is informed by irony. It's second major character is a runaway Negro slave, Jim, who tries to escape to freedom and, unwittingly travels downstream deeper and deeper into the south. Some scholars have been very critical of this matter, and the slapstick ending with the *deus ex machina* of Jim's having been freed by his owner all the time. If we consider the matter of absurdity, however, we can see that this trip into the very heartland has existential implications. Jim moves into the eye of the hurricane, so to speak, and the one from which he can expose slavery's barbarism best.

Twain's irony is apparent in his very first paragraph, a "Notice":

> Persons attempting to find a motive in this narrative will be prosecuted; persons attempting to find a moral in it will be banished; persons attempting to find a plot in it will be shot.
>
> ### BY ORDER OF THE AUTHOR[2]

By disclaiming serious intent and by using the device of humor, Twain is then able to show the meanness, hypocrisy, and hatred in American life without fear of rebuke. Huck functions as a *fool,* and because of his youth and innocence is not held responsible for his comments. The irony in the above passage makes use of the humor of pattern and exaggeration, techniques used throughout the book.

The very name of the leading character is funny: Huckleberry Finn. Huckleberry has a country flavor to it and suggests something quite down to earth, something quite ordinary. He is aptly named for he *is* ordinary and common, and he has a great deal of common sense which is constantly coming in conflict with the various mad and perverse preoccupations of his society: slavery, blood feuds, fanaticism, and so forth. Huck is a good pragmatist, though he is somewhat swayed by Tom Sawyer who has his head full of romantic pipedreams and ideology. In the much argued about ending of the book, which spoofs romanticism, there is a confrontation between Huck and Tom about how to rescue

Jim. Huck wants to dig Jim out with picks and shovels but Tom argues that this cannot be done. They *must* use case-knives.

"Confound it, it's foolish, Tom," says Huck.

"It don't make no difference how foolish it is, it's the *right* way— and it's the regular way. And there ain't no *other* way, that *I* ever heard of, and I've read all the books that gives any information about these things."[3]

It might take thirty-seven years, Tom adds, but that's the correct way to do things. He is a formalist in every sense of the word; a machine, Bergson would say, who cannot adapt himself to situations.

Eventually Tom decides to use picks and *pretend* they used knives, which satisfies Huck, who is interested, primarily, in getting the job done. As he puts it:

When I start in to steal a nigger, or a watermelon, or a Sunday-school book, I ain't no ways particular how it's done so it's done. What I want is my nigger; or what I want is my watermelon; or what I want is my Sunday-school book; and if a pick's the handiest thing, that's the thing I'm going to dig that nigger or that watermelon or that Sunday-school book out with; and I don't give a dead rat what the authorities thinks about it, nuther.[4]

Huck is a good American—he adapts himself to the situation and isn't swayed by "authorities." He is his own authority, and the use of the term is most significant. As a pragmatist, Huck puts things to the test: for example, he tries praying for fishhooks, but when nothing happens he decides that prayer isn't worth very much, or as he said, "No, says I to myself, there ain't nothing in it." He refuses to believe in "spiritual gifts" that are the fruits of prayer and so he "lets it go."[5]

There is a good deal of ridicule of religion in the book. Twain satirizes religious revivals, superstitions, and the supposed morality of many conventional people. Huck wasn't allowed to smoke, but the Widow Douglas, who "learned" him about "Moses and the Bulrushers" took snuff. As Huck ironically pointed out, "that was all right, because she done it herself."[6] Much of the criticism escaped notice because of Twain's tricks—Huck's bad grammar and his youthfulness—but they were there and quite obvious to later generations.

Twain also attacked the royalty and the pretentious code of Southern Chivalry, both of which elicited awe from many naive Americans. When the two charlatans announce, one after the other, that they are of royal blood, a Duke and a Dauphin, no less, Jim and Huck are "overcome." The Duke's description of his plight is ludicrous and mocks romantic conventions: ". . . The second son of the late duke seized the titles and estates—the infant real duke was ignored. I am the lineal descendant of the infant—I am the rightful Duke of Bridgewater; and here am I, forlorn, torn from my high estate, hunted of men, despised by the cold world, ragged, worn, heartbroken, and degraded to the companionship of felons on a raft.''[7] When the Duke starts getting royal treatment from Huck and Jim, the second charlatan announces that he too is of royal blood: "Yes, my friend, it is too true—your eyes is lookin' at this very moment on the pore disappeared Dauphin, Looy the Seventeen, son of Looy the Sixteen and Marry Antonette.''[8] Huck realizes right away that they both are frauds and humbugs, but he keeps quiet so as to prevent friction and avoid trouble.

There are a number of techniques operating here. We have imposters *who do not realize* that they have been "discovered." There is comic rhetoric as well as misspellings, poor grammar, and the revelation of ignorance. As in all cases of imposture and impersonation there is a tension set up: will the confidence men be discovered or will they succeed? In the course of their adventures, the Duke and Dauphin pull off their "nonesuch," a gag that is a practical joke, technically, yet it moves close to the Theatre of the Absurd in its crass stupidity.

The Duke and the Dauphin present a show for men only in which nothing happens except that the Dauphin parades around for a few minutes nude. The description of this is beautiful:

> When the place couldn't hold no more, the duke he quit tending door and went around the back way and come onto the stage and stood up before the curtin and made a little speech, and praised up this tragedy, and said it was the most thrillingest one that ever was; and so he went on a-bragging about the tragedy, and about Edmund Kean the Elder, which was to play the principal part in it; and at last when he'd got everybody's expectations up high enough, he rolled up the curtain, and the next minute the king come a-prancing out on all fours, naked; and he was painted all over, ring-streaked-and-striped, all sorts of colors, as splendid as a rainbow. And—but never mind the rest of his outfit; it was just wild, but it was awful funny. The people most killed themselves laughing; and when the king got done capering and capered off behind the scenes, they roared and clapped and stormed and haw-hawed till he come back and done it over again, and after that they made him do it another time.[9]

After that, the curtain was let down, ending the "nonesuch." The audience was very angry but rather than admitting they had been taken, they decided to talk-up the nonesuch and continue the joke on their townsfolk. The second night other townsfolk were there and also were taken. The third night, the audiences from the first two nights were there with plenty of ripe fruit, but the Duke and Dauphin didn't come on stage at all; they took off on the raft having made almost five hundred dollars.

This little episode is a commentary on the duplicity of people and on the bubble of reputation. The townsfolk were used by the confidence men, who anticipated what would happen, being apt judges of human nature. When Jim comments to Huck that the kings are "rapscallions," it sets the stage for a mangling of history by Huck, who relates how all kings are no good. He tells Jim:

> You read about them once—you'll see. Look at Henry the Eight; this 'n' 's a Sunday-School Superintendent to *him*. And look at Charles Second, and Louis Fourteen, and Louis Fifteen, and James Second, and Edward Second, and Richard Third, and forty more; besides all them Saxon heptarchies that used to rip around so in old times and raise Cain. My, you ought to seen Old Henry the Eight when he was in bloom. He *was* a blossom. He used to marry a new wife everyday, and chop off her head next morning. And he would do it just as indifferent as if he was ordering up eggs. 'Fetch up Nell Gwynn,' he says. They fetch her up. Next morning, 'Chop off her head.'[10]

He continues on with his exposition on the lives of kings, and Jim comments that just living with a Duke and Dauphin is all he can stand.

To this Huck replies, "Sometimes I wish we could hear of a country that's out of kings."[11] And he adds, as an aside, that it wouldn't do any good to tell Jim that the Duke and Dauphin were frauds, *especially since they weren't too far removed from the real kind.* The American democrat is speaking here: no man is better than any other, and those who claim to be superior are usually much worse than their fellow men.

But if the upper classes and their pretentions are shown as ugly and immoral, the same applies to lower-class people; Pop, for example, is a drunken brute. There are also a number of comments about life in small towns, where people are mean and vicious. The whole story has a touch of pessimism and despair about it, except that Huck's resourcefulness and humanity dominates the book and shows the possibilities in American life for men of good will. We need not always submit to the pressures of society and distort our values. As a realist, Huck sees the meanness and selfishness of people, and often plays upon these attributes to save Jim, but there is another side to human nature, best exemplified by Huck, which does not lead to despair. Huck symbolizes man's possibilities for goodness, and Huck's moral development is a demonstration of man's potentialities for goodness being realized.

At the same time that we find realism in *Huckleberry Finn,* we find absurdity and alienation and other existential concerns. If the book is read as an "ordinary" story, even if we do marvel at Twain's virtuosity with the vernacular and comic genius, of course we have features which "mar" it. The trip down into slavery, Huck's alienation from society, the problems of identity that are raised, and the development of Huck's moral character (and personality in general) all can be explained, however, if we look at the book from an existential framework.

I have already said something about how absurdity justifies Jim's trip in the wrong direction and describes the nonesuch; both of these matters have an existential dimension. I could also add something about the liberties taken with logic. Jim's abuse of logic is not far removed from what we find in Ionesco's *Bald Soprano*. In the Ionesco play, some people sitting in a room hear the doorbell, but when they go to the door no one is there. This happens three times, so one of the characters concludes that when the doorbell rings, it is because nobody is there. In the chapter "Was Solomon Wise," the following discussion takes place place between Huck and Jim. Huck has just told Jim that "Polly'voo-franzy" is the way Frenchmen say "Do you speak French?" Jim thinks this is ridiculous and Huck tries to explain why Frenchmen speak French:

> "Looky here, Jim; does a cat talk like we do?"
>
> "No, a cat don't."
>
> "Well, does a cow?"
>
> "No, a cow don't nuther."
>
> "Does a cat talk like a cow, or a cow talk like a cat?"
>
> "No, dey don't."
>
> "It's natural and right for 'em to talk different each other, ain't it?"
>
> "Course."
>
> "And ain't it natural and right for a cat and a cow to talk different from *us*?"
>
> "Why, mos' sholy it is."
>
> "Well, then, why ain't it natural and right for a *Frenchman* to talk different from us? You answer me that?"

Jim's rebuttal is brilliant:

> "Is a cat a man, Huck?"
>
> "No."
>
> "Well, den, dey ain't no sense in a cat talkin like a man. Is a cow a man?—er is a cow a cat?"
>
> "No, she ain't either of them."

"Well, den she ain't got no business to talk like either one er the yuther of 'em. Is a Frenchman a man?"

"Yes."

"*Well*, den! Dad blame it, why doan he *talk* like a man? You answer me dat!"[12]

This passage, with all its mixed up logic and misunderstandings, is as much a satire on logic and the dialectic process as is the nonsense in *The Bald Soprano* about experience teaching people that when the doorbell rings nobody is there. I would suggest that just as Twain's use of the vernacular is an affront to refined sensibilities (and a means toward the most extended kind of social criticism), his absurdities and illogicalities are not elements which weaken the story, but strengthen it.

In the same manner, Huck's famous *alienation* from society has been much commented upon. It is argued that in the ending we have no adequate solution to the problem of how a person of good will is to relate to a corrupt society—other than by flight—and that Twain offers no suggestions or alternative to what he finds. But I do not feel that it is the province of literature to offer political alternatives to situations it finds morally reprehensible. It is enough to point out the evils, for this act suggests the need for reform. Huck's relation to society and his famous statement that he is going to "light out for the territory ahead of the rest, because Aunt Sally she's going to adopt me and sivilize me, and I can't stand it. I been there before,"[13] can be explained in several ways.

First, there is the westering impulse of the Frontier, where one could find opportunity and, we can assume, a better moral climate than existed in society. Huck has seen enough of society not to want much more of it. The escape to Nature is a dominant motif in American literature and thought. The corruptions of Europe and of American society can be avoided; one can reject history which gives the world Henry the Eight, Dukes and Dauphins, and start a new, moral "natural" society.

Second, on a level one step beyond that of consciousness, there is a mythological dimension to seeking out a new territory. When Huck "lights out" for a new territory, he is moving from a profane experience, society, to a sacred one, the new territory. It is often remarked that *Huckleberry Finn* is an initiation story, but this initiation extends beyond merely teaching Huck about life and death. When he lights out, he moves into myth, develops a stature suitable for one who has been on the river, the "brown god."

Mircea Eliade explains the significance of the new territory concept in his remarkable study *The Sacred and The Profane:* "An unknown, foreign, and unoccupied territory (which often means, 'unoccupied by our people') still shares in the fluid and larval modality of chaos. By occupying it and, above all by settling it, man symbolically transforms it into a cosmos through a ritual repetition of the cosmogony.''[14] Settling in a territory is the same thing as consecrating it, Eliade adds, so that one becomes in touch with absolute reality, the reality of the sacred, that is. When one inhabits this new territory and consecrates it, he moves into what is called "The Center of the World." There are an infinite number of Centers of the World, because they do not represent geometrical space but *existential* space.

We can even satisfy those critics who see the quest theme as dominant in American literature—and to be sure there is a quest in *Huckleberry Finn,* though it is for something a bit less tangible than the Holy Grail. Eliade reminds us that: "Those who have chosen the Quest, the road that leads to the Center, must abandon any kind of family and social situation, any 'nest,' and devote themselves wholly to 'walking' toward the supreme truth, which in highly evolved religions is synonymous with the Hidden God, the Deus absconditus.''[15] Huck's initiation and his quest are one—he must probe the nature of the universe, and to do this must light out for the territories where he will be *enlightened.* His initiation into life (and not just into society) is incomplete, his rite of passage down the river, through the "straight and narrow gate" does not end when he is "born again" as Tom Sawyer. Huckleberry Finn cannot stop until he becomes "educated" in the most complete sense of the term.

There is a great deal of death in *Huckleberry Finn,* which is characteristic of initiation rites: "In the scenarios of initiations the symbolism of birth is almost always found side by side with that of death. In initiatory contexts death signifies passing beyond the profane, unsanctified condition. . . . The mystery of initiation gradually reveals to the novice the true dimensions of existence; by introducing him to the sacred, it obliges him to assume the responsibility that goes with being a man.''[16] The book is an initiation rite and as such leads on to its logical conclusion, the discovery of self and the growth and responsibility that stems from this awareness. When Huck moves on, then, he is not so much escaping from society as moving into the center of things, into the Center of The World where he will be a master of reality. In this respect, Huck's actions are paradigmatic of the essential American experience, from the old frontier to the New Frontier.

The *alienation* from society, then, is not a symptom of personality loss but of Huck's authenticity; after all, doesn't he have a classical "I-Thou" relationship with Jim? When we understand the "sacred" significance of Huck's actions, they are not as absurd as they might seem. Directly related to the matter of alienation and the development of "authenticity" is that of *identity,* the last of my existentialist concerns.

The book is permeated by disguises, impersonations, and fabrications.

Huck disguises himself as a girl, impersonates Tom Sawyer, and pretends (and lies) his way in and out of a thousand situations; two bums *become* a "Duke" and a "Dauphin" and they in turn pretend to be other people in the course of their activities; Tom pretends to be "Sid," his brother. The circle of pretence and fabrication is all-encompassing. Huck's impersonations, especially that of Tom, has been interpreted as part of the "death and rebirth" myth, which adds even more evidence to my analysis of Huck as a mythic character. Impersonations are also a standard technique of comedy, and are a technique that has great philosophic significance, for they raise the question of how much we can trust our senses and the whole apparatus of knowing, and how secure our *personae* are. After all, if our identities can be appropriated so easily, and we can be fooled so often, it must mean something?

We learn that we must be skeptical. This does not mean that we must doubt everyting, for absolute skepticism is untenable: if you doubt everything you end up doubting doubt. What Huck Finn suggests is something entirely different, perhaps what might be called an awareness of the possibility of error. This is important, for if we are aware of error then we can try to correct it, both on the individual level and on the social level. We must learn to question ourselves, our assumptions, our values, and the society which embodies them. Things need not be the way they are, Twain shows us, as he spotlights people who are not what they think they are or who others think they are. It is a plea to "resk the truth," in Twain's words. It is very much an American "thing."

NOTES

1. Constance Rourke, *American Humor* (New York, 1931), p. 9.
2. Mark Twain, *Huckleberry Finn* (New York, 1960), no page given in book.
3. Ibid., p. 310.
4. Ibid., p. 310.
5. Ibid., p. 15.
6. Ibid., p. 3.
7. Ibid., p. 157.
8. Ibid., p. 159.
9. Ibid., pp. 193-94.
10. Ibid., p. 197.
11. Ibid., p. 199.
12. Ibid., p. 103.
13. Ibid., p. 374.
14. Mircea Eliade, *The Sacred and The Profane* (New York, 1961), p. 31.
15. Ibid., p. 184.
16. Ibid., p. 191.

The Great Game of Academic

While *The Great Game of Academic* cannot lay claim to being the national pastime, the fact is that it is played with great earnestness by hundreds of thousands of people—all of whom are professors or administrators in our institutions of higher learning—in all parts of the country.

The game is quite simple: following some follower of Doubleday who classified baseball into major and minor leagues, I will do the same for universities. There are *major universities* (and university systems) and *minor universities,* including institutions such as state universities, state colleges, colleges and community colleges. The object of the game is to move from a minor to a major university. This is not easy because people in major universities try to prevent you from doing this.

In fact, and this is one of the difficult things in *The Great Game of Academic,* there is no way to move from a minor to a major university, which means that it is an extremely frustrating game to play. Of course, people do move from minor to major universities every once in a while, but the number of people who do so is so small as to be statistically unimportant.

The nice thing about this game, however, is that it enables people in minor universities to "do" things people in major universities do, and for those in major universities, there is the chance to do a bit of vicarious slumming.

The rules of the game are simple, You cast some dice and add the numbers you get. Then choose the kind of university you are *not* employed in and have a vicarious fling at a different academic life-style.

MAJOR UNIVERSITY

2. Start work on a major work. (Take at least five years to do it!)
3. Take a major offer for more money to the dean.
4. Take a sabbatical leave to Majorca.

5. Fail a Ph.D. candidate.

6. Edit a reader with essays by your friends (who have edited readers with essays by you).

7. Send a letter to an applicant from a minor university refusing him a job and send a letter to a friend who is a "star" at a major university asking him if he's interested in coming to your school.

8. Deny someone tenure and send him to a minor university or second-level major one.

9. Refuse six deanships and two presidencies of state colleges.

10. Get a major grant (Guggenheim, Ford, etc.).

11. Marry your research assistant.

12. Take a Fulbright to a major European university.

MINOR UNIVERSITY

2. Edit a reader for junior colleges and lower-division students.

3. Write a brilliant essay that revolutionizes all previous thought and wait for an offer from a major university, which will not come.

4. Write an essay arguing that teaching is more important, more democratic, more selfless than research.

5. Read an essay telling how monstrous life is at the major universities due to the pressure to write major works every five years, do major research, and keep a step ahead of all the brilliant graduate students. (Only graduate students at major universities are entitled to consider themselves brilliant. If they weren't brilliant they wouldn't be there [which cannot be said of many rich but stupid undergraduate students at major universities].)

6. Give a worthless Ph.D. and make your graduate students work harder for it than at the major universities.

7. Start a new journal and accept material only from people at major universities.

8. Become a campus character.

9. Get the title of your institution changed to the next higher designation until you become either a state university or university.

10. Become a dean, and make offers to "stars" at major universities.

11. Attend a convention and have $300 worth of textbooks sent to you.

12. Try to get a job at a major university as (any or all of): potential genius, token radical, token ethnic, black, or female.

It is quite obvious that life in major and minor universities is unbearable, which explains why we now have so many graduate students and Ph.D.'s who cannot find jobs. The only things that people in major and minor universities agree upon is that no matter where they are and what they earn, they are underpaid. This is because the average professor at any institution of higher learning works between 84 and 96 hours per week, even though his teaching "load" may only be 3 or 6 hours per week. Between keeping up with the literature in his field and playing major or minor university, there is little time for anything else.

Part 6

Fads, Foods, and Artifacts

Status in Foods, or Cuisines as Codes

Recently, a book was published in London listing cheap places to eat; the criterion was, to put it bluntly, "how much food for how little cost." Its title, *Fuel Food,* captures an attitude towards food that many people have. Food is fuel for the body-machine, and food's basic function is to keep us going so we can work hard, play hard, and do whatever it is we care to do.

From this point of view, eating is not a source of sensual pleasure and delight but is, instead, functional and obligatory. This fuelish notion is, I would suggest, a residue of ascetic Protestantism, which has shaped our minds to a great extent, and now we discover, our bodies. Our attitudes in America have been influenced by our Puritan heritage, which has not only affected our sexuality but also our food preferences.

In a remarkable essay called "Gastrosophy" (the philosophy of food), the celebrated Mexican poet and writer Octavio Paz investigated this matter and came to some fascinating conclusions. The adjectives he uses to describe our food tell his story. Our cuisine, he says, is "simple," "spiceless," "honest," and based on "exclusions," just like our culture. Our food "ignores ambiguity and ambivalence," and our beverages (such as gin and whiskey) accentuate "withdrawal" and "unsociability."

Paz compares American food with Mexican and French food, both of which he says involve blendings, transubstantiations, and mysteries. Compared to these cuisines, American food, with its emphasis on purity and passion for milk and ice cream (pregenital innocence), is rather tasteless and bland. We might say, also, that *in America dining has been replaced by eating.* Instead of meals being socializing experiences and happy occasions, we tend to look upon meals as interruptions. There are millions of families who hardly ever eat a meal together; people grab what they can in passing and nobody in the family sees one another, around the dining-room table or anyplace else for that matter.

The whole fast-food industry represents, if you think about it, an attitude towards food—and the mechanization and technologizing of food has a grimness and alienating quality about it that is profoundly disturbing to many people. On the other hand, there is an increasing interest in gourmet cooking, but this is limited, it seems, to small, educated, "sophisticated" elements in the population. And even the lovers of gourmet food treat good dining as something exceptional.

Attitudes toward food are essentially cultural. English food is, as a rule, undistinguished at best, and eating seems to be unimportant to the English—while twelve miles across the channel, the French seem to have made eating one of the focal points of their lives. Statistics show that the French spend more time eating—an average of 106 minutes a day—than anyone else. They also spend a lot of time sleeping (time spent sleeping correlates with time spent eating), leading some to describe the French as having an "eat-sleep" culture.

Although we seldom think about it, every person carries around in his head attitudes and beliefs about food that determine how and what he eats. We all have certain codes and principles of organization that we use when we plan a meal. That is what a cuisine is. We pick up, *though we are unaware of it,* preferences and rules of combinations which affect what we eat. For example, though the English eat great quantities of brussels sprouts and carrots and fried fish, you do not see "fish and sprouts" shops or "fish and carrots" shops, because we all know that chips go with fried fish and nothing else. Americans seldom eat boiled potatos with steak and never boil steak—though it is possible to boil steak, it is inconceivable. Why? Because it violates our codes about what is proper to do with fresh red meat that is tender enough to broil.

Different foods and different kinds of foods have different statuses. When people are invited out to dinner, it is not unusual for them to speculate about what will be served. I know I generally do this. The reason we do so is to determine how highly our company is valued, how much esteem we are to be granted. Generally speaking I would suggest the following chart distinguishes between high and low status foods in America:

STATUS OF FOODS IN AMERICA

High Status Foods	Low Status Foods
whole items that can be carved	pieces of food already cut up or ground
red meat (steak, roast beef)	white meat (chicken, fish)
uncommon (pheasant)	common (chicken)
served natural	served covered with gravy or sauce
large	small
homemade	bottled or canned
identity kept	identity disguised (turned into something else)
individual preferences count (rare)	mass production
bloody	no blood

According to this scheme, roast beef and steak have very high ratings while stews and hamburger dishes have relatively low status, and duck or pheasant, being uncommon, has more status than chicken. When gourmet cooking is involved, the ranking system doesn't work perfectly because we have now introduced a foreign element into our considerations. Veal, which is highly regarded in Europe, is not esteemed here, and if you serve your guests a dish using veal, they will find it difficult to estimate what you think of them. Veal confounds.

This matter of deciding the status of meals is frequently taken care of for us in restaurants; there the price of the item gives it its status and what you order gives you your status in the waiter's mind. In fancy restaurants where waiters are often tyrants and snobs, they exert a great deal of pressure on us to order expensive dishes and prove that we "belong." Unfortunately, as many of us keep finding out, in gourmet restaurants in America, we tend to consume "style" rather than superb food.

Although food is one of those subjects most people tend to take for granted, it is a subject of immense importance. Anthropologists have been engaged in food research for many years and many are now involved "with deciphering" meals, analyzing them in terms of their principles of organization and not in terms of kinds of foods served. Thus meals can be studied in terms of their constituent elements: sours and sweets, solids and liquids, hards and softs, raw food and cooked food—and the way these elements are combined. (From this point of view, the traditional meal of roast beef, roast potatoes and peas is a study in circles of varying diameters. I assume here that one is not a millionaire who can afford a standing rib roast.)

If you think food is important, you must look at the supermarket in an entirely different way. It is not a store, but rather a *mass medium* of staggering cultural significance. (It "broadcasts" food in the same manner that McDonald's, Burger King, Jack in the Box, Taco Bell, etc. broadcast dinners.)

The fact that both the supermarkets and fast-food joints are "broadcasting" so much hamburger has great significance. I call this *hamburgeoisement* of the masses—fooling people into believing they have eaten meat and are middle-class and post-modern. Here we find the digestive system and the socioeconomic system meeting in the hamburger system. Interestingly enough, the supermarkets have come to realize that their main competitors now are not other supermarkets chains but fast food outlets, which are grabbing more and more of our food dollars. Safeway may be McDonalds's neighbor, but it isn't their friend.

Yanqui Bread:
The Great White Way

When I was growing up (in a neighborhood that would now be described as "ethnic"), we used to call white bread "American bread." We ate German pumpernickel, Russian rye, bagels, French and Italian bread—bread that was substantial and that had qualities. American bread was the cotton-like stuff that we used for toast in the morning, or that we played with before Play Doh was invented.

But for most Americans, it is white bread that they grow up on, white bread that they use to create that classic and ubiquitous American institution, the peanut-butter-and-jelly sandwich. White bread is almost devoid of nutrition so the bakers have to add vitamins to it—I believe they do this by spraying it as it moves along on the conveyor belts. In addition, they add preservatives so the average loaf of white bread is really a chemical fabrication, a synthetic monstrosity.

"You are what you eat," said the philospher, and if that is true, we must give thought to what it means to have a population full of eaters of white bread. Once, of course, white bread was reserved for royalty: only the wealthy could afford it. Now everyone can, though I believe the psychic and digestive cost is too great for anyone.

Chemical white bread reigns supreme in the American cuisine, a symbol of the triumph of illusion over reality. For white bread can hardly be said to exist. If you squeeze it you can roll a loaf up into a little mass not much larger than a golf ball. When you let it go it springs back into place! What resilience! What pep! (Is it being built into us with every slice?)

It is this rubberoid quality that is frequently featured in advertisements. American housewives squeeze the bread to see whether it is soft and spongy. And this is the secret of its meaning. White bread is anti-ideological bread—it stands for nothing, it is supremely flexible, it is the embodiment of the American philosophy. Notice that it has no crust. Not on your life.

Crust is antithetical to the American mind, for crust is ideological; it refuses to budge. You can crack it but it will not willingly bend.

Thus the genius of the American bakery industry is to have created a bread that has no crust, no character, no identity. It is an abstraction that merges with whatever it finds itself next to, a non-intrusive elemental that we hardly notice because it hardly exists. It is almost a Platonic conception.

There is another aspect of this bread worth considering—its relation to time. Preservatives are added so as to keep it fresh and soft, so white bread strives to be eternal. White bread signifies our triumph over the forces of decay. Time shall not harden nor harm this loaf, for it is impervious and timeless. It has, like the Americans who devour it, escaped from history.

White bread is also a symbol of the domination of the machine over the spirit, and in this case, over the stomach of modern man—or, at least, the modern American. White bread is manufactured in gigantic super-bakeries that produce hundreds of thousands of loaves each day. There is no human touch to this bread, no stamp of an individual who bakes it; it is just one more assembly-line product made to certain specifications and churned out by the millions. Even housewives never get to touch it until they have purchased it and brought it home.

This bread is a manifestation of all the depersonalization and dehumanization to be found in American society at this time. Each loaf is practically machine-tooled. How can people who eat this stuff (and stuff is a good word for it . . . it is a stuff that we use to take up space in our stomachs or in the stomachs of our turkeys) be expected to be individuals, to have spirit, to have integrity?

We live in an age of synthetic and imitation foods, in which the soybean has become a hero with a thousand flavors. It has been found that rats get more nourishment from the cardboard boxes in which some cereals are packed than the cereal itself. When bakers make digestible plastic wrappers, this will probably be true of white bread, also.

It is a rather curious thing, if you think about it. Most of the countries of the Western world have excellent breads. And yet America, a nation of immigrants from these countries, persists in eating this doughy atrocity. I believe we do so because it helps us to affirm our American-ness. With white bread we repudiate the past and our ethnicity. The blandness of the white bread we eat mirrors the blandness of the society we have created.

White bread is third-generation bread, a bread for people who have lost their accents, their taste, and in too many cases, alas, their souls.

Some Thoughts on Threads

Clothes have always interested me. Actually, they interest most people—since everyone, except for an occasional nudist or streaker, has to find something to wear each day. We get dressed and undressed so often that the significance of clothes—and fashion, in particular—tends to escape us.

The average person has no theory of fashion; all he or she knows is that it is important to be fashionable, to look good. There are some people who do use fashion for particular purposes; there are style rebels and there are "ego-screamers" who use clothes to call attention to themselves. But most of us pay little conscious attention to what we wear once we've made the decision to purchase and wear certain clothes.

But what is *fashion*? Why has denim "caught on" so much in recent years, and why are women wearing pants?

Fashion is a mode of communication. Every day when we get dressed, we are presenting ourselves to the world and others are going to judge us by what we wear. Our clothes create impressions and give other people ideas about who and what we are. Once clothes were pretty good indicators of class and status, but with the development of what I call "denimization" and the general trend toward the leisure look, clothes don't make the man so much as hide him. A lot of people seem to be hiding in denims and other kinds of clothes whose basic virtue is that they *don't* tell much about the person wearing them.

Most of us have a subliminal understanding of fashion's power to communicate. What many of us do not understand is how it works. Why does one pair of denims look ludicrous, all of a sudden? And why does another pair look great? We all know what we like, but often we don't know why.

Fashion is constantly changing. Most people, I believe, wish to be relatively inconspicuous. If they don't change with the fashions, they will stand out.

Although an individual chooses the specific items that make up his wardrobe, the decisions he makes have, in a sense, already been made for him. He will select from a range of possibilities open to him. The basis of his selection will stem from social and cultural pressures exerted upon him in a subliminal (or not so subliminal) manner. If you ask him why he is wearing an outfit of faded denims, for example, he will tell you that his outfit looks "good" and makes him "feel good." But he won't know why.

Many of us have illusions about our capacity to decide things for ourselves in modern society. While I believe people do have a measure of freedom, the very existence of "styles" and "fashions" suggests that people can be swept away and carried along in certain ways. Fashion is, after all, a form of collective behavior. The "individual" choices that many people make are often choices to go along with millions of others in wearing rugby shirts or coveralls or whatever.

How is this change generated? In aristocratic societies, the styles were set by the nobility. In democratic societies, the source of fashion changes is harder to locate. It may lie with our substitute royalty—our celebrities, actors, actresses, entertainers, sports heroes and heroines, and so on. But whatever the case, you have to change to keep in style.

In a society with egalitarian values such as ours, there is great pressure on people *not* to be different, not to "put on airs" or act superior. Denim has become a symbol of some kind of cultural revolution that is taking place, that we are all dressing like the working class. But there is another explanation. That is that denimization reflects the aping of the rich by middle-class people, that the rich are now rejecting conspicuous consumption and so the middle-classes are dressing poor too.

In recent years, denim has escaped from its "work clothes" identity, where there was no fashion involved; some denim clothing is now relatively expensive. Denim has become a universally popular fabric whose very blandness leads some people to decorate their denim jackets and pants and skirts in all kinds of elaborate ways. The decorated denims reflect a desire that people have to personalize their clothes, to strike some kind of a balance between the anonymity of mass produced garments and the need for individuality.

Sometimes this need for something unique leads to style anarchy. Fashion becomes completely disconnected from its social role (of telling us a person's status), leading to what might be called "stylelessness." This is what we get when everyone is doing his own fashion thing. It is not an indication of individuality but of social confusion. Nobody knows who anyone is anymore or how to dress. Since society is based upon communication and people being clear about their roles and other people's roles, stylelessness creates confusion. Stylelessness is self-defeating, since when everyone is competing for attention by dressing unusually, nobody gets noticed.

Most of my female students now wear pants to class. When I ask them why, they all give me the same answer: "Pants are more comfortable." They also tend to laugh when I suggest that pants have been traditionally worn by men (at least in the Western world), and that women wearing pants are symbols of the desexualization that is taking place in American society. A good case can be made that men are dressing in more feminized styles (frilly shirts, silky fabrics) and women are dressing in more masculine ways (pant suits, the "jock look," etc.). This would indicate that sexual identity is getting all mixed up.

Although it is a complicated matter, I can't help but think that the masculine fashions women are adopting are based upon a loss of sexual identity rather than upon comfort. Fashion is not based on utility and ease but on display, among other things. There is also the matter of homosexual fashion designers, who might be expected to masculinize women and feminize men. In the case of desexualization, fashion reflects important changes going on and helps accelerate the changes as well.

Many people mistakenly assume that fashion is a trivial phenomenon with little impact on our lives. Yet the clothes we wear play an integral role in our development; the messages we send with our dress are instrumental in our developing a sense of who we are.

The notion that our fashion or dress is instrumental in the shaping of our identities explains the stress many people feel when they shop for clothes. We realize when we buy some article of clothing that people will be making judgments about us on the basis of its appearance. One of the appeals of Levi's, for example, is that is "top of the line," and the various little tabs and symbols Levi's uses are all calculated to communicate this. Brooks Brothers and some of the other established clothing stores use the same appeal. When you buy at Brooks Brothers you are buying history and tradition and an identity—something to the effect that you are a man of "quality."

I have an uncle who has worn clothes from Brooks Brothers for fifty years. He always said he wanted to look like a man who might be "the president of Princeton." My uncle never went to Princeton or any other college. He looks like he did, though. He appreciates, more than most of us, the aesthetic and sensuous qualities of clothing. What we wear does have an effect on our sense of ourselves and our feelings. You feel different about yourself when you are wearing an expensive shirt than when you are wearing an inexpensive one.

Many people buy clothes when they feel depressed. The question is why? One reason for this—and this applies to housewives in particular—is that shopping for clothes is an excursion into the world at large and a means of escaping from "the house," which often takes on the characteristics of a prison. We often purchase clothes as a kind of *reward* we feel we are due, after traumas or achievements, when we believe we deserve something nice. But the most important reason for purchasing clothes to ward off depression is that a new outfit implies, psychological-ly speaking, a new self. New clothes allow us to be born again and to escape from the anger and guilt we felt about our "old" selves.

We all probably have certain articles of clothing we wear when we are in certain moods, though we are not aware that we are wearing these items because we feel the way we do. Maybe when we are "roaring mad" about something we wear a certain suit and then proceed to give people hell.

A young woman I know who is a schizophrenic told me that just before she has psychotic episodes she wears a certain bright yellow dress. It was a sign that she was about "to drop off the deep end," as she put it, which she didn't recognize for a long time.

The point of all this is that the clothes we wear—our threads—are deeply involved with our feelings and our psyches.

Why is it that the clothes we loved last year look so terribly silly and old one year later? Why does everyone have such a passion for cotton denim? And why are women wearing pants and coveralls sometimes and micro-bikinis other times?

Could it be that the "threads" we wear are, in some strange way, like the threads that are attached to the arms and legs of marionettes? Do the "threads" that cover us also control us?

Varieties of Topless Experience

> When we see all things in God, and refer all things to Him, we
> read in common matters superior expressions of meaning.
>
> Here then is the psychological foundation from which symbolism
> arises. In God nothing is empty of sense: *nihil vacuum neque sine
> signo apud Deum,* said Saint Irenaeus. So the conviction of a
> transcendental meaning in all things seeks to formulate itself.
>
> J. Huizinga, *The Waning of the Middle Ages*

THE VISION FROM HEAVEN

She comes "floating down from the heavens" on a $3,000 grand
piano. First you see her legs, turning and twisting, as the band blasts out
wild rock-and-roll rhythms. Gradually the rest of her body comes into
view, glistening in the bright lights, and you see her breasts. They are
enormous, and for a good reason. They have been enlarged by silicone
injections to become super-breasts, objects of reverence in a breast-crazy
culture. You can't make up your mind—are they grotesque?

"And now," shouts the band leader, "Miss Carol Doda will perform
the swim!" With that, her eyes flashing, she starts some gyrations for a
minute or two, and then she stops. As she does, the lights start flickering
so that the performance takes on an ethereal quality. She freezes between
each rendition. When the next dance number is announced, the bright
lights turn on again and she performs; this is followed, once more, by the
flickering lights. She becomes, once more, a vision...she's there, she
isn't, she's there. After about ten minutes of dancing she is pulled up into
"the heavens" and her performance is over. The audience applauds,
then leaves.

Topless dancing, as it is called in San Francisco, started at the Condor,
with Carol Doda, on June 16, 1965. According to Dave Rosenberg, the

public relations director of the Condor who thought up the idea, it was inspired by topless bathing suits that Rudi Gernreich made so popular, and by his seeing a picture of a little four-year-old girl (also topless) in the *San Francisco Chronicle.* "Do you want to pack the club?" he said to his bosses—"If you do, let's have Carol perform in a topless bathing suit instead of what she is wearing now." The idea caught on big. Now some fifteen night clubs in San Francisco have gone "topless."

There is a certain magic to the term (which has packed the Condor and a number of other clubs—attendance is up to 100 percent due to it) and yet, really, it is a very confusing one. On the most obvious level, topless means without any clothing on the top, or barebreasted. Yet it also suggests unparalleled (i.e., "can't be topped") and, ironically, less up top. This latter meaning is not very apropos if you consider that all the topless stars have 39-inch busts, thanks to silicone injections.

Carol Doda says she loves dancing with bare breasts, that she feels it is an art form. "It is the most personal way that I can communicate with people," she says, "and as far as bare breasts are concerned, let's face it—sex is a part of life and we can't hide it." She is a rather short blonde—if not by nature then by inclination—who comes from the Napa Valley. Although not well-educated, not having finished high school, she is quite articulate and even has intellectual inclinations. Six times a day, seven days a week, fifty-two weeks a year she dances. She is beginning to find it hard to come to work and is also somewhat anxious to get on with her career, to become "big" as they put it in the entertainment world, and make a name for herself. But the Condor has invested a great deal of money in her and she is under contract, so for the time being, she must remain where she is is. The audiences at the Condor will be seeing those visions of celestial beauty, if you consider her beautiful, for some time to come. Without her the attendance would drop, for she is a star attraction, and they come to see her, or her breasts, and for no other reason. She is the only dancer in the Condor who is topless, the only person at the Condor who is topless.

When I saw her performance, I was impressed by the ritualistic quality of the whole thing. After all, her name, Carol, means to praise, she is a "star" who descends to the stage as if she were some kind of heavenly spirit, and the lighting turns her into some kind of vision. And of course, dance is a traditional form of worship. The only thing is the new religion is one of some kind of mixed-up cross between Dionysian sex and mother worship. A woman's breasts in America are symbols of sexiness—the voluptuary with great cleavage—and are also symbols of "mother." The standard joke in topless places involves a customer asking a topless waitress for some cream in his coffee.

It is hard to account for the importance of big breasts in America.

Why, for example, do they stand for sex *rather than* mother here? Why is the American cultural ideal of the sexpot a woman with large breasts while, for instance, in Argentina, Burma, Japan, and numerous other countries, big breasts are frowned upon and often made smaller by plastic surgeons? Before I answer this, let's take a look at another topless dancer, the featured dancer of "Big Al's," Tara.

TARA: THE FOOL OF GOD

Tara has a much different style from Carol Doda's, and she is somewhat of a joker. They both have a glassy look in their eyes when they dance, as if the exhibiting of their breasts and the beat of the music were giving them some kind of sexual thrill, but whereas Carol Doda's performance is highly stylized, ritualized almost, Tara seems to be making fun of the whole thing. She is a better dancer than Carol Doda and bumps and grinds in the tradition of burlesque queens. What is most intriguing about Tara's dancing, however, is the way she controls her breasts and uses them in a comic manner. She bumps them together, she makes them spin, she makes them wiggle—she is then a master comic, as I see it, a fool of God.

Her life is rather austere. She doesn't drink, she doesn't smoke (except at work, where she gets nervous and bored), and also performs every day of the week. Between her performances, which last only five minutes, she sleeps in a little room in the cellar. It is almost as if she were in a holy order—living in a cell except when called, hourly, in this case, for her devotions. Three days a week she works out in a gym to keep her figure, and she is on a very strict diet, because if her figure "goes" she'll be out of a job. She is not a big "star" like Carol Doda and does not have great ambitions. "I think it's great," she said about her job, "but I don't get excited or anything like that when I dance. It's just a way of making a living." The reason it is popular, she says, is that the topless gives people a chance to see something they think they shouldn't, that it gives them a feeling of getting away with something. "The men," she says, "like to compare me with their wives. They watch the show with more or less blank looks on their faces. The women tend to have a nervous smile, so as to seem calm, but really they are terribly jealous and often make catty comments afterwards."

The reason the men don't become sexually aroused, she says, is that they realize thay "can't do anything about it" if they are, so they more or less refuse to let themselves go. Tara is an intelligent girl and has many ideas about what the topless signifies. She sees it as a hallmark of what she calls the "sexual revolution" that she sees taking place in the United States. "Women weren't supposed to enjoy sex up until recently," she said, "but that has changed. They want it and they are getting it. It isn't such a big thing to go to bed with a man anymore."

What does all this breast-worshipping mean? Why should we be so intoxicated by breasts; why should these artificially bloated breasts pack the nightclubs the way they do? The topless isn't as sensuous as the strip—there is no dramatic development and little suggestiveness to it, and the dances are usually very short, because the audiences have short attention spans. "Once you've seen one you've seen them all," said a doorman at one of the clubs.

As I see it, the topless is an American contribution to religious dance, perhaps even a type of Marianism jazzed up to rock and roll which attempts to expiate overwhelming Oedipal forces in American society. In this ritual exorcism, the topless dancer is mother as sexless sex goddess, and with her we finally get to have the equivalent of the peek into the bedroom. If we can't "have" a mother, we can at least get her out of our system this way. With Carol Doda, mother is a vision, celestial and untouchable; with Tara, she is a fool of God, who makes us laugh our way into some kind of God-intoxicated hysteria.

When I left the Condor the band was playing "Get Me to the Church on Time." It is a strange new religious development, this topless—a uniquely American contribution to the cult of the Virgin.

Part 7

Amongst the UK

Hamburger Heaven

Ten years ago, when I had my very first McDonald's hamburger, I sensed that somehow I was in the presence of an enormous force, an institution of awesome energy. McDonald's hamburger is, it turns out, an evangelical hamburger, a hamburger with grandiose territorial ambitions as well as divine zeal. In the course of the last decade, it has become the dominant "fast-food" franchise in America—and it is now spreading abroad, carrying its gospel of machine technology wedded to cheap hamburgers wherever it can find a mouth-hold, and converting anyone it can to the glories of junk food, American style.

The genius of the McDonald's hamburger is organization, rationalization, and specialization. This is all carried to the point of perfection, so that the consumer can have his hamburger with the minimum delay and at the cheapest price possible. There is now even a McDonald's "university," where McDonald's owners are taught how to operate their restaurants super-efficiently. These franchises, which offer a very restricted menu, work on a continuous flow format, something like an automobile assemply line—with hamburgers being cooked continually, and everything else being at the ready, so that orders are completed almost at once. The secret is being able to estimate demand so that no hamburgers are wasted—not an impossibility, because the McDonald's operation is supremely efficient.

Below the individual mouth lurks the mass stomach, and McDonald's understands this stomach more than anybody else in America. McDonald's offers a machine-tooled hamburger, a hamburger that is, in truth, more of an abstraction than a reality, one that is all essence and without corporeality. What do you expect for 20 cents (8p)? Meat? You do not eat a McDonald's hamburger because you are hungry—though four or five of them and some chips might fill you up. You eat them because McDonald's offers immediate gratification (no waiting). When you eat a McDonald's hamburger, you feel that you are part of America and in communion with all the vital forces at work there.

You do not get this feeling when you eat a Wimpyburger. Wimpy provides an undistinguished, perhaps even a regrettable hamburger. I've only had one. It was a thin wafer of meat, pale grey verging on brown, that lay uncomfortably upon a few fried onions. The roll which enclosed it had the faintest hint of a crust and was just slightly more substantial than the McDonald's cotton fluff roll. But we must remember that the Wimpyburger at 16½ p for a take-away hamburger costs twice as much as its American over-the-counterpart.

My hamburger had a coarse grain and two extras: it had a large piece of gristle in it, as well as (somehow) a piece of thread about two inches long. I had ordered one takeout Wimpyburger, and as the cook passed it to me in a small bag, I had none of the feeling you get at a McDonald's. Wimpy is not really a fast-food house; it is a restaurant chain that happens to sell lousy hamburgers. (I don't know what the other food is like at Wimpy's, but I'm not tempted to try my luck there again.)

The restaurant chain is named after a gluttonous character in the famous American comic strip, *Popeye,* and that's just about as far as the Wimpy Bar or Wimpy House goes in terms of resembling anything "American." In America, the fast-food joints are plastic all right, but they are authentically and outrageously plastic; they take delight in their vulgarity and push it, at times, to the point of being art. Wimpy, on the other hand, and its competitors in Britain have a diluted garishness that is not, in any way, exciting. Wimpy doesn't have the symbolic richness that McDonald's does—it doesn't carry any psychological baggage and does not confer any psychic rewards upon its customers.

And relatively speaking, the essential Wimpyburger is frightfully expensive. You don't get much value for money. There are, of course, all kinds of hamburgers—depending upon what you want to pay for them. In London now, there are many American hamburger joints which offer thick, charcoal-broiled hamburgers, but they are not hamburgers for the mass man, for the person in a hurry or the insolvent student, or the man without qualities who wants a hamburger without qualities.

Wimpy offers a rudimentary hamburger devoid of condiments, except for the onions. McDonald's, on the other hand, insists you take your hamburger with a prescribed mixture of mustard, ketchup and relish, though I've heard that if you protest, you can get a plain hamburger. But there is more to the hamburger than meets the eye, and Wimpy and McDonald's have a grander significance.

I am referring to the *hamburgeoisement* of the masses. The automated hamburger is marching, ineluctably, and threatens to overwhelm the traditional cuisine of the Western world. The hamburger (and other fast foods) is changing people's eating habits and, with this, the whole social fabric that has been constructed around these eating patterns. The basic political function of the automated hamburger is mystification—fooling people into believing that they have eaten meat (like the fancy people do) and making them think they are post-modern.

In America and probably in Britain, people eat more meat than ever before. But statistics show that, since the Second World War, Americans are eating much less steak and other prime cuts and much more hamburger—so in truth their standard of living has gone down. The fast-food franchise is the last hope of the so-called "little American" to rise in the world. Most of the growth in the American economy is in the service industries, but there is so much competition between hamburger joints or hamburger mansions (some are quite fancy) that the hamburger no longer guarantees wealth and success. All too often, on both the individual and social level, it only leads to heartache and heartburn.

What I have been trying to suggest is that McDonald and Wimpy hamburgers must be seen as more than just hamburgers. They are potent symbols which comprehend within them whole societies, economic systems, world views, and so on.

Remarkable, isn't it, what you can find in chopped meat, sometimes?

London's Underground
As A Work of Art

There is probably no work of art that strangers in London spend more time looking at then the map of the London Underground, designed by one Paul E. Garbutt.

Native Londoners or people who lived there a long time and who travel on the underground have memorized or internalized large sections of it, and don't have to bother with it; but for others, it is a diagram of compelling interest.

Actually, it isn't a map, since it was consciously designed and is diagrammatic rather than representational. If is formal and abstract—perhaps both a piece of hard-edge realism (out of the Mondrian school) and a functional tool.

There is no concern with streets or with scale, and yet the diagram is terrifically powerful. This may be because it presents the logic of the London Underground and is total—it "comprehends" so to speak the entire system, which is enormous.

The London Transport calls it a "Diagram of Lines" (which sounds plebeian yet which has an art nouveau ring about it), but it is quite obviously much more than that. The roundel, the circle with a line through it, is a potent symbol—a kind of variation on the Chinese Yin and Yang symbol—and the diagram itself, covering about 250 miles of track, is a model of economy and functionality.

The roundel is a symbol of undergroundness in general and the diagram is a symbol, at a lower level of abstraction, of the underground as an entity or as a system with its eight different lines, interchanges, etc. The diagram is both a symbol and a guide and provides what might be called representational mastery.

To understand the scope of this system, you might compare it with the Bay Area Rapid Transit (BART) in the San Francisco-Oakland area, which will have 75 miles of track and which hopes to function (if they can ever get it finished and working properly) as a regional transportation system.

The statistics provided by the London Transport are impressive:

Mileage in tunnel—99.

Longest tunnel—17miles.

Longest nonstop trip—34.1 miles

Number of stations—279.

Speed—20.3 m.p.h.

The figure for speed is not impressive; however, when contrasted with the average speed of buses in London (11.3 miles per hour) it doesn't seem too bad.

Now what is remarkable is that all of the above is "comprehended in innumerable printed diagrams of every size and coloration, provided by London transport, tourist guides, etc. The diagram gives mastery and power; it is functional and provides one with the illusion of control, somehow, of this vast entity.

Of course, this sense of power is contingent; you can only go where the transport goes, and, especially in the north of London, it is hard to get from one place to another.

For example, if you wish to go from Hampsted, on the Northern line, to Wembley Park, on the Bakerloo line, you must go nine stops south on the Northern line to pick up a train and go 12 stops north on the Waterloo line. Yet Hampstead and Wembley Park are quite near one another.

The key to the underground is the interchange system. Since the underground was not built as one system, but represents a merger of a number of formerly separate ones, it contains numerous redundancies. It is held together by the interchanges which connect one, two, or three of the eight different lines.

In a sense, the underground is really a regional system, since its focus is in bringing people into the center of London and getting them about in the downtown area of the city, and not in facilitating their getting about in the extremities. There are something like forty interchanges, and most of them are located in or near the central loop formed by the Circle line (and at times the District and Metropolitan lines).

Despite the redundancies and certain inconveniences, the underground is an effective system.

It serves as a reference point for people; you tell people where you live by citing the nearest underground station, and this station becomes part of a person's identity, actually. A person who lives near the Hampstead tube is perceived as (if not really) different from a person who lives near Elephant and Castle.

The tube stop becomes a central point in knowing the location of restaurants, cinemas, theatres and museums. In part this is because it is hard to drive in London and find places to park, but also because of the power of the Underground Diagram to place things in people's minds.

Think of it. The greater London area has a population that is probably in excess of ten million people, and yet the locations of most places in this city are presented in a highly abstract and formalized diagram that often is no larger than four by six inches.

A vast and complicated system serving ten million people presented in a simple little diagram which enables anyone to understand it in moments.

Though it takes hardly any time to master the diagram, it often takes a good deal of time to get from one place to another, which demonstrates that the Underground Diagram confers the illusion—but not the reality —of power. Because we understand the system we think we control it. Knowledge may be power—but not in the case of the London Underground.

Upstairs, Downstairs

[*Upstairs, Downstairs,* a production of London Weekend Television, is produced for the Public Broadcasting Service as part of the Masterpiece Theatre series by WGBH, Boston. Directed by Cyril Coke et al.]

Americans have long defined themselves as middle class. We believe we have a "classless" middle-class society, with small fringes of people on either side—the fabulously wealthy and the desperately poor—but they are anachronisms. This sense of classlessness leads to a great deal of anxiety and restlessness. Since we never can be sure where we are on the social scale, we do not know how to act or what is proper.

That is why the *Upstairs, Downstairs* series, which has been running on the Public Broadcasting Service (PBS) for two seasons, is so comforting to Americans. We are so concerned about being "masterless" people that it is a relief to see individuals who know precisely who they are and what they can expect out of life. The world of *Upstairs, Downstairs* is that of two distinct classes—the wealthy and the poor, the masters (who dwell upstairs) and their servants (who live downstairs) in the Bellamy household in Edwardian England. It is very binary, reducing English society to its extremes and presenting a point of view devoid of middle-class influence. Perhaps Americans, who are feverishly "upward-mobile," take pleasure in seeing people who are not. Each character has his place in the great chain of being and is reconciled to it.

The differences between upstairs and downstairs people can be explored as follows:

Upstairs	Downstairs
Wealthy	Poor
Masters (command)	Servants (obey)
Educated (but often silly)	Not educated (but often shrewd)
Leisure	Hard work
Openness	Closure
Space	Crowdedness
Champagne	Beer
Marriage and infidelity	Bachelorhood and spinsterhood

Although they have different perspectives and inhabit different worlds, the relations between masters and servants are dignified and proper on all sides. There is respect all around and the servants' dignity is admirable. That is the irony of it all, as far as Americans are concerned. Americans serve no one, but experience a strong sense of alienation and deindividuation. Because we respect nobody, nobody respects us and our supposed freedom offers little but isolation. This may be because identity in America is so involved with negation, with being men and women sans categories. Curious that the English working classes, hemmed in and without the sense of mobility of the American middle class, are so beautifully defined and have so much identity. It is almost as if the chains that bind them (in our view of things) also support them. Thus, an Englishman like Hudson, the butler, exudes a kind of security and strength that we cannot help but admire. The average middle-class American identifies with the people upstairs, obviously, but he does not really have their style and certainly not their manners.

The fundamental theme in the series, the difference between the wealthy and the poor, is reflected in almost every episode. The superiority of the wealthy does not extend to the realm of morality. The upper class is portrayed as being bored, infantile, and venal, particularly on weekends in the country. It is the servants who hold their lives together, just as it is the working classes who are exploited and who create the vast wealth that the rich squander. A Jewish businessman confides to Captain James Bellamy (son of Richard Bellamy, who is a member of Parliament), as they observe the goings-on at the country house both are visiting, that he would put a gun to his head rather than lead the empty life typical of this class.

Yet, for all their frivolity and lassitude, the young men had a sense of duty and honor that was commendable, as shown in the episode about the outbreak of World War I. They did not recognize the immensity of the forces at work, but bravely raced in to do their duty. They ran off to war as if it were a continuation of their garden party, but for people whose lives were garden parties, such is to be expected.

In the series, the upper class gives the masses security; that is, after all, what is most important to the working classes and to the people downstairs. In one episode, when the household seems on the verge of disintegration and Captain James is not sleeping with his wife Hazel anymore, fighting breaks out among the servants. As Daisy, the maid, says, "I don't feel safe anymore." The title of the series emphasizes social distance, but though the house must be, as Captain James tells Hazel, "run with dignity from upstairs," the lives of masters and servants are connected and merge together. The moral of this is that when rulers lose control, the masses are plunged into chaos.

The Bellamy household is obviously a microcosm which represents a macrocosm—England. The marriage of James Bellamy to Hazel Forrest, Richard Bellamy's former typist, takes on symbolic significance. James has married "beneath" him, and the clarity that had characterized all relations between the two classes is now clouded. When those upstairs and those downstairs maintained proper relations, based upon respect and deference, England was sure of itself and life was harmonious. When the essential simplicity of the situation was destroyed, the stage was set for tumult.

The fearful and conservative element of the working class—Hudson for example—expected the worst. Hudson believed that James had made a great mistake in marrying Hazel and blamed her for household troubles. Rose, head house parlor maid, disagreed and told Hudson he was living in the past. "She had the chance," Rose said, "and she took it." The immediate cause of the difficulties was Hazel's miscarriage, which drove James from her. On a personal level, this reflects his infantile personality; she had deprived him of a toy that he wanted, and this led him to turn his attention elsewhere. On a cultural level, it means that James, as a member of the ruling classes, recognized that he had made a fatal error: the bloodline was contaminated, the progeny would not exist or certainly would not be the same. When downstairs sleeps with upstairs on the marriage bed, the old way is doomed. In effect, the story of James and Hazel is a parable about the dissolution of the English way of life just before World War I.

In *Upstairs, Downstairs* the controlling matter is the resolution of the dialectic, which is central to the series. Characters find themselves in all kinds of situations, people fall in and out of love, there are personal tragedies and social cataclysms, but pervading everything are the two-class oppositions, forming a background against which figures play out their lives. In America, we have resolved the dialectic, for better or worse, and we are curious about England. We have escaped from history and in so doing, escaped from domination by people upstairs. For all practical purposes, we have fallen between the two domains and have expanded our stake on the stairway until it dominates the house. Still, we have notions that life upstairs may be more interesting and turn our eyes in that direction. While we ponder the future and the dialectic, one thing is certain: knowing how to type is useful.

The Pub Life is Changing

Does "Malt do more than Milton can—To justify the ways of God to man" in England? I'm not sure such is the case, but it does seem quite evident that beer plays an important part in the psyche (and social life) of the average Englishman.

In this sense, it is analogous to milk for the average American, for both confer psychic rewards and are intimately connected with the development of young people in the two countries. Americans drink a great deal of beer but though, as the ads used to proclaim, "beer belongs" in America, it is not as important or central as in England.

After the American has been weaned from milk, there is a latency period and he begins with alcoholic beverages—beer and then hard liquor. The Englishman, on the other hand, tends to stay with beer, and it is beer that is the "organizing" beverage around which the pub is constructed, and upon which much working-class (and other) socializing revolves.

The public house, the public parlor—for people who have none, or skimpy ones—is connected with certain basic myths about England: mateship, conviviality, maybe even courage (the name of a popular beer). And now that the saloon bar and public bar have merged, England is ready to proclaim itself, silently, that is, in its own imagination, on the verge of being a classless middle-class nation like America.

Beer used to be, so everyone tells me, much better in the old days—it had body, it had character, it had strength. Now the traditional British malt beverages—bitter, brown ale, and stout (which everyone tells me is "good for you and very nourishing") are under attack from thinner, lighter, more "refined" lagers.

And as the beer gets thinner and less wholesome, the *ongoing party* (which is what a pub is, especially for its locals) loses its centrality, and the myth of England, as a land of stout-filled stout-hearted lads, fades. Conversation can't compete with the telly, and canned beer is cheaper, anyway.

The pubs are not dead by any means, and when you go to one you are quite likely to find it buzzing, but it is not the center of the action in the social life of the working-class man to the extent it was.

Pubs are now getting more expensive, as television sets become cheaper. A recent article in one of the London newspapers said that many Englishmen will not be able to afford both cigarettes and beer and will have to choose one or the other.

In England, beer is seen as connected with virility, power, strength, and manhood. A recent ad for Double Diamond showed a man at the end of his first day off cigarettes, weakening as he inhaled fumes from other people who were smoking. Fortunately for him he got a pint of Double Diamond, and as he drank it, in an enormous and almost orgasmic swallow, his resolution firmed immediately. It made all the difference.

If it was the playing fields of Eton that created the upper-class heroes who preserved democracy and provided leadership to the masses, it was the pubs of England that the bone-weary masses retreated to, to repair their bodies and give their spirits a lift, with beer that had body and character.

Those days have now passed; the English public schools are no longer full of people who assume they are born to rule, and the pubs are not full of people who can be led by the nose and who can find solace only in strong beer.

There is a theory which suggests that the working classes are becoming middle class and that this is a clever trick by the capitalists, who wish to "buy off" the masses by giving them a stake in society. This theory of embourgeoisement might explain the inroads which lager has made in England.

The working classes, now with a petit-bourgeois mentality, have their stake (and kidney pie) in society and imitate the middle-class types by drinking lighter beer and even hard liquor from time to time.

Beer, then, does justify the ways of God and the ruling party to man in England—and there is little likelihood of a revolution as long as the working classes have their beers, their birds, and their boob tubes.

English Encounters

A YEAR AMONGST THE UK:
AN ANTHROPOLOGICAL EXTRAVAGANZA

I don't know how it was that I ended up amongst the UK, but circumstances led me to live with them and observe their various and sundry rituals (as Malinowski said, "ritual is always rite"), to study their dominant myths, to chart their everyday activities—in short to do what any fieldworker does when living amongst strange peoples. The UK, once a savage and bloodthirsty people, are now relatively civilized. They are found on two rain-soaked islands, near the continent of Eur, and are much ridiculed by the people in Eur for their habit of boiling meat and serving beer warm.

The UK are a confederation comprising four tribes: the *Eng* (known for their strange little black derbies which they call bowlers), the *Sco* (famous because the men wear skirts), the *Wa,* and *NIrl.* Although these four tribes speak the same language, Englingua, because of the incredible variations in the way they speak it, many of them cannot understand one another. Still, there are certain phrases that are universally used, such as "Gaw Blimey" and "Wot?" and "here, here", sometimes pronounced, "'ere, 'ere."

One of the favorite pastimes of the UK is in telling myths and legends about their kings and queens. One king is said to have had eight wives; when one displeased him he had her head cut off. ("Off with your maidenhead" he said. Then, "Off with your head maiden."). A war was supposedly fought over which end of the egg—the big end or the little end—one opens when eating a soft boiled egg. The UK like nothing better than going to plays about their kings and seeing them cut their wives' heads off and throw one another into dungeons.

The islands on which the UK live are full of old castles and fortresses, and people visit them to see the dungeons where various kings, queens, princes, and bishops were imprisoned and killed. That was the national sport before the development of *roc* and *soc,* their two preoccupations now. The UK still have a king and queen, mostly to dedicate underground stations and endorse brands of marmalade and tinned peas. All kings and queens have to love horses or else they are thrown into a dungeon.

In the old days, the kings and their friends, the royalty, used to ride around covered in tin cans and have tournaments, in which they would poke at each other with big sticks or try to hack one another to bits with long metals things which were primitive forms of can openers. One king who liked round tables is especially famous for having killed numerous dragons and monsters that used to inhabit the land. (He was so successful that none are to be seen at this time.)

The sport which the UK follow most passionately, *soc,* is not unique to them, though they presume themselves to be the best soc players in the world. Soc is a sport in which people kick a round ball all about a big field and chase it about, and hit it a great deal with their heads. It is here that the thick heads of the UK are a great advantage.

Old *soc* players are generally thrown in dungeons and beheaded, so many resign when young and become milkmen, butchers and, if lucky, plumbers. When the UK lost a big soc match to a rival tribe, the Pol, one of their papers had for a headline, "The End of the World!"

The UK worship a god who is, they imagine, very much like themselves, in that he speaks Englingua and takes boiled water and leaves (tea) at ten in the morning and four in the afternoon. They worship this god in big buildings which they erected many years ago, and which hardly anybody visits now except tourists (who want to see where certain kings were killed) and lonely old ladies. These halls are convenient places to purchase postcards and catch cold.

Now the UK no longer build big buildings for their god, but build big *soc* stadiums and airports. This is so people who wish to fly to visit the UK and see where UK kings were killed can do so easily. (The most famous place to see dungeons and where more kings, queens, ladies, and little boys were killed is called the Tower, and many people visit it each year.) In the soc stadiums, the best soc players in UK run around for ninety minutes and manage to score one or two goals, sometimes three, during a game. The soc stadiums are also used for *roc* concerts in which bands of school leavers and functional illiterates play electric guitars and entertain young girls, known as teenyboppers and teenyweenieboppers, and young men know as mods, rockers, and skinheads.

The UK are notorious for having sour dispositions, which accounts for their loving candy, or as they call them, "sweets." Also, the UK are terrible gossips and say the most terrible things about one another at their morning and afternoon teas. They also believe in beating children in schools with canes and birch branches. At the age of eleven, all children are given futures by the teachers—some are sent off to Oxbridge, a famous university where they are required to punt, play a game called rugger, and write books of philosophy. Others are sent off to be milkmen, dustmen, and bobbies.

When not delivering milk or picking up dust, these types—in the working classes, as they call themselves—play soc or indulge in their favorite pastime "go wn'out." They assemble in huge mobs, carry signs, and make speeches. Since the working classes and the Oxbridgeans who run the country speak different Englingua, the have to spend a good deal of time talking to one another before they understand each other. While all this is going on, the PriMi and the MOP's, who operate the government while the king and queen are opening subways and eating marmalade, make speeches and have meetings and drive around in big black limousines, called Minis.

UK women are notoriously ugly. Some have long thin noses that wiggle while they speak; others have snub noses and mousey features. (They all manage to get married, however, because they can boil meat.) They consider it fashionable to wear rags and old garments which they get from dustmen. A few wear skirts called micro-minis, which are, in reality, skirts they used to wear in the third form. The only good looking women in UK are the *au pair* girls, imported from all over the world to look after UK children while their mothers are out washing their horses' behinds, attending charity teas, or selling fish.

Some of the UK, whose great-grandparents were usually crooks and swindlers, and who are rich, love to chase foxes. The UK do not believe it is fair to have one UK chase one fox—since foxes are notoriously clever. Therefore, usually fifty UK mounted on horseback and one hundred hounds chase a fox—to equalize the odds. The hunt ends when the dogs tear the fox to pieces, after which the UKs on the hunt have tea and cucumber sandwiches, discuss the UK's glorious heritage and various interesting problems of moral philosophy, and complain about the cost of servants.

It is best to have gone to Oxbridge and studied linguistic philosophy if you wish to chase foxes, though the very best preparation is to join the Queen's Guard after Oxbridge and march around in little soldier suits and learn how to be wooden soldiers. The Queen's Guard protect her while she is in the kitchen eating bread and honey and on her way to underground stations. After the Queen's Guard, Oxbridgers marry girls who have studied poetry and ballet in fancy private academies called Comprehensive Schools and go into business to make a fortune, so they can wear top hats when they chase foxes.

All in all, I would have to say the UK are amongst the most crazy people on the face of the earth, and certainly the most pernicious—at least as far as foxes are concerned.

A REVELATION ABOUT ROYALTY

As an American, I have always found the notion of *real* kings and queens to be quite strange. When I was a child, I heard countless fairy tales about kings and queens and assumed that they were proper and suitable in the old days, but in modern times? There is, of course, an egalitarian ethos in America that makes us feel very uncomfortable about what we could call "all this royalty nonsense." The idea that there are lords and ladies, counts, barons, princes and princesses, dukes and duchesses, etc., etc., is okay for the fairy tales but not for real life. We prefer our princes to be princes of commerce, men who have achieved things on their own and not on the basis of a kind of "selective breeding."

There are many in England who feel the same way, though statistics show that the royal family is very popular, and the recent marriage of Princess Anne received elaborate media coverage and most of the English people felt very happy about the matter. The Republicans made great jest about the two partners, neither of whom seem particulary interesting or in any way remarkable. They share, it seems, a passion for horses and not very much else.

England now is a country which only maintains the illusions of power, and a royal family is needed to help sustain the illusion. They are a very special kind of theatrical performers, who are kept busy with numerous social engagements and lend a kind of dignity to opening dams and underground stations, and that kind of thing. The Queen is rather matronly and sexless, but seems to be a decent enough person, though not remarkable in any way except one—she is the Queen.

Why, then, do the English keep a royal family? There are a number of reasons behind it. First, they have had kings and queens for a long time and anything that is traditional in England has considerable value—if only for pulling in the tourists. Pope said "whatever *is,* is right," and most of the English would agree with this, except that they might add whatever *was* also. (I am excluding social and political legislation from this discussion, though I should point out that they have been much more creative than Americans in some regards.)

Secondly, there seems to be a certain amount of sense in separating political power from moral and symbolic power. In America, the president's family is the *first* family and the president is looked upon as a symbol of all that is great (and conversely, at times, evil) about America. Having a person who is a symbolic leader and not also the political leader is a good solution to this problem, though this can be done without a king or queen.

The real reason, I suspect, for having royalty is that it is possible, then, to print those wonderful "By Appointment" symbols on jars of marmalade or cans of green beans. These symbols confer great security and many other gratifications to the English public (as well as the Danish one and all others that have royal families). There is no problem of anxiety about what kind of ham to buy. For a few pence more you get the kind the King of Denmark eats, and that should be good enough for anyone. The "By Appointment" symbols are guarantees of propriety—and hopefully, of quality.

They also, in a subtle way, imply *equality,* since if we are what we eat, and we all eat items with "By Appointment" symbols on them, we are all the same, even if we don't all live in Buckingham Palace. Thus the Englishman is offered equality in the sphere of consumption, and the royal family can be looked upon, in this regard, as idols of consumption.

This points up a tangential function of the royal family. They solidify and define lines of status and remove doubts as to where one belongs (or what one eats when one wants "the best"). As a result of this, you find a remarkable sense of assurance in English aristocratic families; they are "born to rule," and find support and confirmation in this, should they ever have a doubt, every time they reach for a jar of raspberry preserves.

The advertising industry plays up on the status conferred by these symbols, and spurious imitations of them which "suggest" the "By Appointment" symbols are found on many cigarette packages which seek to assure smokers that they are smoking quality cigarettes. What all of this proves is you don't have to be a king to live (almost) like one—though you may need a king's ransom!

THE QUEEN'S TOY SOLDIERS: ARE THEY LUCKY STIFFS?

During the first part of my stay in England, I took my family to see the Changing of the Guard. It was mobbed—with tourists from all over the world, who were packed solid around the gates and across the street on various statues and the steps leading to the Mall. Platoons of camera-laden Japanese flowed about, and you could hear German, Spanish, and any number of languages being spoken.

Why all these people were there is a question that interests me. Everyone knows, of course, that "the British know how to put on a good show," and the Changing of the Guard has a hint of splendor and grandeur about it, but I find it a very thin event and not worth the effort it took to get to Buckingham Palace. It is free and that may account for its wide popularity.

There was one thing that struck me, however, and that was a guard inside the palace grounds who stood at attention without moving (so it seemed) as much as an eyelid. He seemed to be frozen into his stance—and might just as well have been a wooden soldier carved by some master craftsman. Many of the tourists standing around, outside the gate, marvelled at him. "How does he do it?" they asked. *A better question might be—what does it mean to have a man turn into a toy soldier?*

To me he symbolized the oppressive weight of tradition and formalism that I sense in England, and a kind of self-control that verges on the pathological. I assume that the men who serve as guards engage in a kind of self-hypnosis that allows them to maintain their rigid position the way they do. But the adjectives one might use to describe these guards are all, ultimately, quite negative: frozen, rigid, like a statue, motionless, etc. There is a ring of morbidity to it all—a kind of rigor mortis, but for the living and not the dead.

Why should guards be rigid and seemingly lifeless? Why should they approximate toy soldiers? Is there any value in having a guard motionless and stiff, like a board? Those guards symbolize and concretize (a good word since they seem to be made of concrete, seem almost to be cast rather than made of flesh and blood) the most negative aspects of English—or, in particular, upper-class English—character, as I see things.

They symbolize the suppression of instinct, of warmth, of humanity. They are like marionettes which have been tossed, by chance, into a certain position, and which remain there until someone pulls a string or two. Self-control is an admirable feature, but carried to such lengths as one finds in the guards, it is monstrous and brutalizing. If, as I have been told, it is considered a great honor to serve in the guard, and an honor more or less reserved for people with "good blood" and Oxbridge educations, then all the worse I say.

Of course I come from a culture which does not have such traditions, which stresses being "down to earth," informal, ordinary, and flexible. In America we believe, as the song goes, in "different strokes for different folks." We don't put on good parades the way the English do, because we know that we have the power and don't need the pomp.

But what we are concerned with is not the power of the guard (except as symbol) but the power of a culture and tradition that leads people to want to become guards and that makes approximating a toy soldier an honor. I will, no doubt, be accused of *reductionism*—of not being aware of the traditions behind the guards, of what their stance signifies, and that sort of thing. One can always make such arguments, but I don't accept the logic. If you have to be a "true believer" to properly understand anything, then nothing will be criticized since "true believers" aren't critical.

These guards, most certainly, are true believers—with as much faith (is that the word?) as any Hindu fakir, who puts himself into a trance. England, I would suggest, needs people who have a sense of the way things are moving and who can help shape that movement: what they get is a genius for standing still becoming one of the highest attributes in their "best" young men.

THE DAILY CALENDAR:
THE FULLY BOOKED LIVES OF THE MIDDLE CLASSES

Recently I attended a meeting of a social committee of an organization which will remain anonymous—a meeting which I found most instructive. There were about a dozen people at the meeting, mostly couples, except for myself. Before I attended the meeting I received an agenda in the mail, and on the evening of the meeting, I received a telephone call to make sure I would be there. Lots of energy at work.

Their first order of business (the reading of the minutes was omitted because the secretary was ill) was a discussion of a questionnaire the committee was sending out, in an effort to find out what social activities members of the organization would be interested in. The matter was complicated, because there was a covering letter starting out "Dear Member" and ending "Yours truly." "Don't you think 'Yours sincerely' would be better?" asked one of the committee members. "No," answered the chairman. "A letter starting out with 'Dear Member' is too impersonal, and I can't sign it 'sincerely.'"

Also, the mailing of 1,300 letters and questionnaires takes a bit of doing and they had to decide how to manage it all. Someone even suggested the whole idea was a bad one. The head of the organization had not cooperated with the venture, it seems. He believed that questionnaires like that were quite useless, a waste of time and money, and an invasion of people's privacy. But the chairman of the committee, a forceful and exuberant individual, was resolved to push on with the project.

Once this matter was out of the way, the committee addressed itself to planning the social calendar for the rest of the year, up to the summer. The committee was not quite certain of its mission—raising money or helping people to get to know one another better, or both. It was decided to have a variety of events, at a number of different price ranges. There was to be a "Brain" game, in which people could answer questions at different tables, on various subjects. There was a lot of talk about how much this should cost.

Originally it was decided upon that it should cost one pound per person. However, the chairman mentioned that people had complained about the cost of events put on by the "Social and Functions Committee," so after a bit of discussion, it was decided to lower the price to 50p per person. I can't recall whether they decided to make another appeal for a certain charitable entity. One member objected to the practice of always making appeals—she thought it would be nice to have something in which people weren't pressured. Someone else, however, argued that the need was desperate, and people could well afford more money.

In addition to the "Brain" evening, the committee decided to have a bridge evening, and a party of some kind. Someone suggested they sponsor a night at the movies, and this was debated at length. Some thought that if an evening of film was held, it should be at the headquarters of the organization. Others felt there shouldn't be an evening of film because it wasn't a socializing experience, and people didn't really mix at such evenings; they merely were together, but no relationships ensued.

The biggest problem of the meeting involved a "culinary experience" that the vice-chairman thought might be a good idea.

"What do you mean by a culinary experience?" one member asked.

"A good feed, in essence," was the reply.

"Can we get really good cooking for a lot of people—I mean, can you have a really good meal that way?"

"That's not necessary," answered another person. "We know a cook who caters meals from time to time . . . she's even cooked for Princess Margaret."

"How much would this cost?"

"Shall we say three pounds per person? That's not too much for a good feed," volunteered the man who had suggested the culinary experience.

The couple who knew the cook suggested they all go to her little restaurant in Hemel Hempstead, but the gas shortage put the damper on that idea. This couple also suggested that going to her restaurant wouldn't give a good idea of her capabilities, because she catered to the relatively unsophisticated tastes of her clientele.

Finally the committee decided to engage her to cater a private dinner party for themselves, so they could see how good she was. People thought that three pounds per person was reasonable, and someone volunteered to host it.

"When shall we have it?" someone asked.

At that, many of the committee members whipped out daily calendars to see when they would be free. It could not be this day because someone had to fly to Bucharest. It could not be another day because a couple were going to Denmark. After a number of stabs at a reasonable date, everyone agreed that they had a free Sunday a month off and plans were made to see what could be done about getting the woman.

The time for the tea break arrived, and several men went down to fetch tea. During this time a number of Irish jokes were told—all based upon the "stupidity" of the Irishman. I gather that the Irishman occupies the same status in the English joke world as the Pole does in the American joke world. The jokes were expertly told and actually quite funny, being absurd and fantastic. Some of them were similar to American moron jokes, also.

After tea time, the committee wrapped things up, set a time for the next meeting, and adjourned.

"Will you be coming?" asked the wife of the chairman.

"Yes," I said. In its odd way, the evening had been quite fascinating, and I wanted to see how things were resolved.

One of the committee members asked me if I needed a lift home, and everyone said good evening to me as I left. I really don't know why I was asked to attend these meetings, except that I got cornered one evening at one of their events and I suppose it was actually a gesture meant to expand my social horizons, so to speak. Originally the meeting was to be held in a private home, and arrangements had been made for me to be picked up and returned.

What impressed me most about the meeting is that it revealed certain aspects of middle-class life that both attract and repel me. The people in the committee were dedicated to providing something constructive for their organization and worked quite hard at their task. They were also all extremely intelligent, and many of them were quite witty. The meeting itself was a rather gay one—lots of gags, comic performances, and joking about, in addition to the Irish jokes, that is.

But the thing that fascinated me most about it was the way so many of the people used their Daily Calendars. The woman sitting beside me had one, and I glanced at it . . . full of things jotted down for each day. The good life is the busy life, and a marked-up scribbled-over Daily Calendar is the sign of the good life.

This *participation hunger* is a kind of aggression—and reflects a hunger for activity that has several motivations. On one hand, it is a kind of assertiveness, a passionate desire to suck the marrow of life as completely as possible. It is a form of greed that manifests itself in a frenzied effort to fully book oneself "into life," in a manner of speaking. I can't help but think that such people are really very lonely and have inadequately developed inner resources. It may be that people who need to be with others all the time can't stand themselves? It may reflect an evasion of the self that we all manage to achieve, one way or the other. The round of daily activities allow us (and perhaps even forces us) to focus our energy and attention on the outside world and prevents us from thinking very much about ourselves. The working classes and the upper classes also practice such evasions; there are many methods—drink, sports, the telly, the cinema, etc., etc. But the important thing is to avoid focusing attention upon the self, upon the self that is lingering there within us, kept down and rendered inaccessible.

We have all heard that inside every fat man there is a thin man, longing to get out. The same thing applies to all of us, though not in terms of being fat but in terms of a submerged self that we occasionally take notice of, but generally keep hidden—from others as well as ourselves. This submerged self asks philosophical questions about the meaning of our lives, the morality of our activities. We avoid this submerged self. Instead of writing books of philosophy, we write up appointments in our Daily Calendars and add up our activities in a calculus of hedonism and self-evasion.

Thus there are several histories of Britain being written at this moment (and histories of every country). There is the official history, of the doings of kings and prime ministers and great artists and military commanders. But there is also the anonymous, petit-bourgeois history being written in all the Daily Calendars printed up by Collins and W. H. Smith, the history of the middle classes. There may also be a history of the working class, and this history may shape the future (if the Marxists are right). But it may also be that the working classes have no history, that they merely *are,* hidden away in the shadows, keeping things going, so the middle classes and the ruling classes can have their social committees and Parliaments.

SHOPPING CARTS, SUPERMARKETS, AND THE SUPERSTRUCTURE

I find that most of the English people have a very strong identification with England, its history and culture. They may be the moral equivalent (nowadays) of peasants, but they seem to think they are blessed by England's glories, and that the existence of royalty and of princes is some kind of a benefit. Of course I am speaking metaphorically here. W. H. Auden has said, "Each in the prison of himself is convinced of his own freedom," and the same could apply to national fantasies. We are all, deep within us, convinced that *our* customs, *our* beliefs, *our* lifestyles, *our* ways of doing things are best.

Thus when I mentioned, in a lecture on one occasion, that I thought that one of the supreme symbols of life in England is the little shopping cart that legions of women drag behind them every day, and that the way people shop in England was wasteful (of time), there was a great outcry in the audience. "What's the hurry?" said one person. "What will you do with the time saved?" "Who likes frozen meat?" asked another. People started making impassioned speeches about the English way of life and why refrigerators aren't necessary.

Comparisons are, of course, odious; there is always the implication of judgment at the very least, and criticism is not palatable to anyone. Yet I must say that I believe the British (and European, for it is not restricted to Britain) way of purchasing food to be quite irrational. Millions of women are out to millions of stores wasting millions of hours every day. Shopping is a way of life in England, and though it has certain values in that it provides a means for socialization and enables women to "get out of the house" for a while, it also means that they are enslaved. Daily shopping is a necessity—you miss a day (or forget about an early closing) and you starve!

England is a nation of shopkeepers, but the other side of that is that it is also a nation of shopgoers. The multiplicity of shops is astonishing . . . and in each shop are large numbers of clerks whose productivity, I would imagine, is relatively low. I must say I find it all rather quaint and in a sense "charming," but it is not very efficient.

The American institution which contrasts with the multiplicity of little shops is the supermarket—though there are now supermarkets here, and even, in fact, an American one—Safeway. Powerful forces have led to the development of the supermarket in America—it is a supremely rationalized institution, it is relatively efficient, it provides numerous services for its customers, it brings together an astonishing assortment of goods under one roof . . . it is the modern equivalent of a street market except that is is located in one building. Supermarkets in America are getting larger and larger now. The typical American supermarket used to stock 4,000 products: it now stocks 10,000 and its volume has grown greatly. The larger the supermarket, the larger the volume (and the volume may increase almost geometrically) and the greater the profits.

The consumer in Britain is under the illusion that all these shops are a convenience for him. In reality he pays dearly for them—in time and money. The shops reflect a kind of anarchy that pervades this country. There is no reason, no order, no organization to speak of. Instead the streets are lined with little shops that replicate each other every five blocks, and for the most part, are not particularly interesting.

Thus the woman out with her cart is a kind of beast of burden—a coolie, a carrier, who is tied to these shops by invisible threads that bind her as securely as if they were steel chains. "My grocer," they say, or "my greengrocer," but this *my* has a kind of reciprocal obligation to it. She "belongs" to them as much, really, as they "belong" to her.

I have a particular animus against these shopping carts because, as wielded by many women, they are often dangerous weapons. I happen to do most of the shopping in England at the local Waitrose (the significance of the name is apparent—you *wait* and by the time you get to the cashier you find the price of everything *rose*) and have been wounded numerous times by these carts. For some reason people seem to bump into each other frequently here; I can't explain it. The supermarket has narrow aisles, for one thing, and people seem to rush about in it, for another. But even outside the market there seems to be little concern for other people's territory.

The shopping cart is a symbol which embraces what might be called the system of consumption and involves, ultimately, the economic system in Britain and the continent. Economics means, literally, the laws of the household—and there is a direct connection between the shopping cart and the household appliances people own (no refrigerator or a miniscule one without a freezing section of any significance means no frozen foods means there is a need each day for fresh food, and so on). In turn, there is a connection between the wages people get, how much they can afford to spend at any one time, and how stores operate. All of this, in turn, relates to the proportion of people who have cars and whether or not supermarkets have parking lots and the way goods are packaged and the kinds of paper bags available.

It may be that the American supermarket represents when pushed to its ultimate a kind of extreme—antiseptic, overwhelming, supremely rationalized, impersonal, institutional, but I do not think this is an accurate picture at all. The gigantic supermarket currently popular in America represents consumption at the highest level of rationality and efficiency, and if it is an extreme, so might I add is the anarchistic continental system of consumption. The supermarket could not function the way it does without the American way of life, the American economy, American affluence, the American passion for efficiency and time-saving.

The supermarket is a generalist institution; the private shopping cart and all it involves is an artifact of a "specialistic" mode of consumption. The shopping cart is for people with tunnel vision, immediate needs, present-mindedness. It is the legacy of the peasant, the little man who makes little purchases. In order to move into the era of the supermarket and all it stands for, there needs to be a wide-ranging revolution all up and down British society; you cannot impose supermarketing as a total system without restructuring the rest of society to go along with it.